The Floral Baker

FRANCES BISSELL is the author of numerous books and was *The Times'* food writer for thirteen years. Her articles have appeared in a wide range of publications in both the British and the international press, including *The New York Times, San Francisco Examiner, Boston Globe, Le Figaro, The South China Morning Post, Bangkok Post* and *El Diario de Jerez*, and magazines such as *Taste, A la Carte, Victoria* and *Food Arts*. She has written and presented two television series based in the West Country and appeared on a variety of TV shows in North America.

She has received the Glenfiddich Award for Cookery Writer of the Year in Britain, while her *Book of Food* won a James Beard Foundation Award in America. Frances Bissell has been guest chef in some of the world's leading hotels and restaurants, including the Café Royal Grill Room in London, the Mandarin Oriental in Hong Kong, the George V in Paris and The Mark in New York. She is a member of the Royal Academy of Culinary Arts.

By the same author

A Cook's Calendar

The Pleasures of Cookery

Ten Dinner Parties for Two

Oriental Flavours

The Book of Food

The Real Meat Cook Book

The Times Cookbook

The Times Book of Vegetarian Cooking

Frances Bissell's West Country Kitchen

The Organic Meat Cookbook

An A–Z of Food and Wine in Plain English
    (with Tom Bissell)

Frances Bissell's Modern Classics

Entertaining

Preserving Nature's Bounty

The Scented Kitchen

The Floral Baker

Cakes, pastries
and breads

Frances Bissell

Serif
London

First published 2014 by
Serif
47 Strahan Road
London E3 5DA

www.serifbooks.co.uk

9 8 7 6 5 4 3 2 1

British Library Cataloguing in Publication Data.
A catalogue record for this book is available from the British Library.

Library of Congress Cataloging-in-Publication Data.
A catalog record for this book is available from the Library of Congress

ISBN: 978 1 897959 54 1

Designed and set in 11pt Bembo by sue@lambledesign.demon.co.uk

Printed on Munken Premium White 80 gsm paper and bound in Malta by
Gutenberg Press Ltd

Contents

For Tom

Preface

Baking is one of the few areas of the culinary repertoire in which we can still find regional distinctiveness, something to be treasured in an era when food has become so similar that we can eat a meal and be uncertain whether we are in Manhattan or London, Paris or Hong Kong. But the fragile pastries, tender *macarons* and buttery brioches of the French *pâtissier*, the voluminous yeasty sweet breads of Austria, Germany and points east, the almost medieval spiced delicacies of Italy and Spain such as *panforte* and *alfajores* are all symbols of that rich diversity, to which must surely be added the fruit cakes and tea breads of the British Isles. How different all of these are to the crisp pastries dripping with honey and filled with almonds and pistachios found in North Africa and the Middle East, and to the sweet caramel smell of freshly baked treacle rings in the tucked-away bakeries of Valletta's side-streets. So let the baking begin, in all its glorious diversity!

Over the years I have been lucky enough to share kitchens with generous cooks who have also shared their recipes with me. My mother taught me to bake, and I learned many recipes from her. Before I was tall enough to reach the work surface, I can remember stirring the Christmas cake batter and being given the baking bowl to scrape out the leftovers with my brother. It was a handsome bowl, huge it seemed to me then, deep, with sloping sides. It was unglazed on the outside and had a creamy yellow glaze inside. For my own Christmas baking, I always use a pot from Gozo my mother gave me, unglazed earthenware outside and glazed white inside, speckled with a soft raspberry pink, a version I have not been able to find since.

In my late mother-in-law Edith's kitchen in Pennsylvania

I learned to bake traditional eastern European yeast breads, particularly the nut roll, yeast dough wrapped round a filling of sweetened ground walnuts. Her sister's version of the yeasty crescents was quite different, made in small, individual sizes, filled not with ground walnuts but with ground poppy seeds. It was in Edith's kitchen that I also learned how to make pumpkin pie, and now, for me, its rich warm spicy smell heralds the holidays as much as the smell of mince pies in the oven.

My travels as a cook have taken me into many professional kitchens, where I have been invited as guest chef on numerous occasions, from the Falkland Islands to the Philippines, from Cairo to Bogota, from Kuwait to Colombo, as well as memorable weeks spent in glamorous hotels in Hong Kong, New York, Paris and London. And in each place, despite the long hours I would put into preparing and cooking traditional British food, I always made time to learn from the chefs and *pâtissiers* with whom I was working. Their skill, artistry and craftsmanship, which I know I could never emulate, always fill me with admiration. And each time I work with them on my recipes, those recipes invariably emerge much improved and with more elegance and refinement.

In retrospect, baking formed much of what I prepared and served abroad, particularly when I was invited to present 'traditional English afternoon tea' promotions. And so I baked scones by the hundred, fruit cakes, Victoria sponges, spiced biscuits and coconut macaroons, saffron buns and lardy cakes, their names alone often an indication of their origin, from the long tradition of using saffron in Cornwall to the practice of using lard for baking right across the English Midlands, where the pig is king. In an article entitled 'In Defence of English Cooking' published in December 1945, George Orwell highlighted saffron buns, as well as treacle tart, plum cake and shortbread, as being uniquely English, although the Scots would surely lay claim to shortbread.

Very early on in my career as a food writer I was commissioned to write a feature for the *Sunday Times* magazine to celebrate the nine-hundredth anniversary of the Domesday Book, a 'what the well-to-do medieval household would be serving for Sunday lunch' piece. This led me straight into our rich culinary archives, amongst them the earliest English cookery manuscript, the thirteenth-century *The Forme of Cury*, considerably later than the period in question, but, of course, foodways changed much more slowly then than they do today. There I discovered the beginnings of the baking traditions in England. My most treasured recipe from the *The Forme of Cury* is for an early version of cheesecake, using honey, saffron and soft cheese, mixed with eggs and baked in a pastry case. This was called *tarte de Bry*, Brie tart, for indeed, not only did we speak Norman French in fourteenth-century England, but we made a soft cheese called Brie.

But baking is not only about tradition; it also offers scope for imagination and innovation which will not tread on any culinary traditionalist toes. You only have to look in a *pâtissier*'s window in Paris to see fantasy and the traditional side by side, towering architectural structures, frivolous, frothy confections, baroque and unusual combinations of flavours next to the more sedate *gâteau St Honoré* and a tray of *financiers*.

And baking has allowed me to indulge in another of my culinary passions, which is the use of flowers and flower scents in the kitchen. As I wrote in this book's predecessor, *The Scented Kitchen*, this is not about using as many edible flowers as possible – it is about using the flower's scent as a flavouring, as one might use a herb or a spice.

The Floral Baker is exactly what the title says, recipes for baked goods of all kinds enhanced with the subtle floral scents of roses, lavender, violets, jasmine and more. In the first chapter I describe how to capture some of the flavours, as well as offer suggestions on commercial preparations. Thereafter, chapters on breads, tea loaves, sponge cakes, biscuits, shortbreads, tarts, fancy pastries and festive baking include recipes for every occasion, from a simple afternoon tea to a wedding, even for those who have never baked before, but are attracted by the idea of capturing the scent of lavender or a rose in a delicate pastry.

Frances Bissell,
London and Gozo 2014

Disclaimer

Whilst the author and publisher have taken all reasonable steps to check the accuracy of the information in this book concerning the edibility of flowers used in the recipes, readers are strongly advised to carry out their own research if using flowers not mentioned in this book.

The author has consulted the National Poisons Information Service and has used as a guide *Poisonous Plants and Fungi* by Marion Cooper, Anthony Johnson and Elizabeth Dauncey, published in 2003 by the Stationery Office, the most accurate and up-to-date guide, in book form, at the time of writing, which she has found to be invaluable. She hereby acknowledges the work of these three specialists as an important source of information. The National Poisons Information Service has also contributed to the compilation of a CD developed by the Royal Botanic Gardens, Kew, which has been produced for doctors and other specialists.

Readers outside Britain are advised to consult their local, regional or state poison information authority for the most up-to-date guide available.

Neither the author nor the publisher can be held responsible for any accident whatsoever which may occur as a result of using this book.

Acknowledgements

I am grateful to all those – friends and family as well as profes-
sionals – who have shared their kitchens with me over many
decades, experiences which have immeasurably improved my
baking. And to the gardeners who have offered me lavender
and roses in season, in abundance, I am also deeply grateful. All
too numerous to mention, they know who they are, but I shall
single out my mother and my late mother-in-law for particular
acknowledgement and loving thanks. Both exceptionally good
bakers, I learned so much from them.

Serif is the nicest publisher I have ever worked with. After
writing *The Scented Kitchen*, I was delighted when Stephen
Hayward agreed to indulge my love of baking, provided it was
contained within my passion for using flowers in the kitchen. So
he has my warmest thanks, as does Rachel Irwin for her timely
prompt. I am grateful to Sue Lamble, as well as Justus Oehler,
Sarah Wilbois and the team at Pentagram's Berlin office, for once
again producing such a handsome book.

Someone had to eat all these cakes. He did a heroic job, in this
and everything else. Thank you, Tom, as always.

Some notes on floral flavours and ingredients

In my earlier book, *The Scented Kitchen: Cooking with Flowers*, I wrote at length about edible flowers and how to use them to make floral jams and jellies, glazes and sugars, creams and butter, but you do not have to prepare all floral flavours from scratch. There are excellent commercial flower waters, essences, alcohols, dried flowers, jams, jellies and syrups available. Some of the more common ones, such as orange flower water and rose essence, can be found in the larger supermarkets, a number of which also now stock own-label lavender sugar. Dried rose petals can be bought from herbalists and health food shops, as well as those specialising in Middle Eastern and Asian ingredients. Dried lavender for culinary purposes is increasingly available, from lavender farms and also from producers of herbs and spices. Saffron is a store-cupboard essential in my kitchen, for both sweet and savoury baking, literally kept in the cupboard, as it should always be stored in a dry, dark place in an airtight container. And, when I can, I collect fresh fennel flowers, as these are perfect combined with cheese and other savoury items in pastries and muffins.

In season, of course, one can find fresh flowers for baking, such as elderflowers, marigolds, nasturtiums and mimosa, all of which add subtle flavours and scents to one's baking.

Herb farms and lavender farms are an excellent source of locally produced edible flowers, including Maddocks Farm in Devon, www.maddocksfarmorganics.co.uk. The Hop Shop in Kent, which can be contacted on www.hopshop.co.uk, produces very fine culinary lavender essences from home-grown English lavender, one for baking and hot dishes and one for creams and ices. If shopping in France, Chabaud C&S from Montpellier produce a wide range of herb, spice and flower extracts. Amongst the cinnamon, basil and lemon grass, I found rose, violet and jasmine in La Grande Epicerie de Paris, www.lagrandeepicerie.com. These come in 15 ml bottles with a dropper and are expensive, but a little goes a long way and I consider them an excellent investment. Saravane, a company based in Arcachon, produces small sprays of *parfum culinaire*, for using as a final touch on desserts, pastries and fruit salads. The Provençal olive oil producer Nicolas Alziari has developed a range of floral syrups, rose, violet and the more unusual mimosa, all of which are available at www.alziari.com.fr. The small *comptoir colonial*-type of shop in Paris and other large French cities is also a good source for floral essences and crystallised petals. The long-established French manufacturer Eric Bur produces flower jellies, including violet, and crystallised petals and seeds such as pink lilac and mimosa.

Considerably less costly than essences and culinary perfumes are floral waters, especially orange flower water, rosewater and occasionally lavender water. These are the by-products from the distillation of essential oils. There are some English manu-facturers of rosewater and orange flower water, but far and away the best I have found are those from the Lebanon, sold in Middle Eastern and Asian food shops, as well as the 'specialist ingredient section' of the larger supermarkets. This is also where I buy Turkish rose petal jam, *gül receli*, quite delicious, and I try to keep a jar on hand, especially in the spring and early summer when my own rose syrups, sugars and glazes have run out.

You will find rose essence, or rose oil, of which you only need a drop or two, in Indian shops, and also rose petal powder, made from dried and ground rose petals. This is an excellent ingredient, which I have used in sponge cakes and rose butter cream. There you will also find the headily fragrant kewra water, an extract from the screwpine or pandanus. The US Star Kay White range of natural essences and flower waters is available in the UK by mail order from Lakeland. Their rose essence is very fine, and a little goes a long way. Lakeland also stocks own-label violet flavouring as well as a range of highly concentrated food colourings. The baking section of Waitrose, Sainsbury's and some other specialist sections of supermarkets stock the Nielsen Massey range of essences, including rose and orange flower.

There are commercially available flower jellies and preserves that can be used in baking – for filling sponge cakes, for example; some of them, inevitably, are better than others. It puzzles me that anyone would think it a good idea to combine lavender and violet in a jelly, however, as each flavour cancels out the other; much better to make your own.

Flower liqueurs, for example the Italian Rosolio, used to be very popular in the nineteenth century. Versions of Rosolio di Rosa are still made today, especially in Sicily, and are worth tracking down when on your travels. Combier, a 150-year-old distillery in Saumur, has revived the art of making flower liqueurs and their Liqueur de Violette and Liqueur de Rose have very pure, intense and natural flavours and aromas that are perfect for flavouring floral butter creams. And anyone visiting Toulouse will want to hunt out the fragrant syrup and crystal-lised petals of the deep purple-blue *violette de Toulouse*.

Some practical advice on cooking with flowers

Do not eat anything that you cannot identify simply because it smells as though it would taste good.

Even if you know a flower to be edible, such as a rose, do not use it for culinary purposes if you think it may have been sprayed with harmful substances such as pesticides. **Flowers purchased from high-street florists or supermarkets should not be used in the kitchen**, as these will almost certainly have undergone spraying and other chemical treatment. You should only eat bought flowers if they come from a florist who can guarantee that they have not been sprayed.

On the question of garden roses, and flowers in general, commercial sprays are out, even organic ones, which often contain toxins such as nicotine. Only innocuous home-made recipes, such as vinegar- or soap-based sprays, are safe for flowers destined for use in the kitchen.

Flowers growing on grass verges may have been exposed to carbon monoxide fumes, animal excrement and other waste, so, however attractive they may seem, they are best left where they are.

It is not advisable to use flowers in the kitchen if you suffer from asthma, hay-fever or other allergies. This includes skin allergies, as handling certain flowers may exacerbate the condition. Some flowers, such as lavender and fennel, have powerful therapeutic properties, and should not be taken in large quantities, especially when pregnant.

Many of the flowers traditionally used in cooking, such as violets, primroses, mallow and cowslips, are wild flowers. The countryside is no longer carpeted with wild flower meadows – those that remain are part of our dwindling natural heritage and should be preserved.

There are certain protected species of wild flowers that cannot be picked. Some people feel that we should not pick any wild flowers, while others believe that, where there is an abundance, a light picking will not cause any harm. Wild flowers should never be uprooted for transplanting to your own garden. It may be illegal to do so; it is certainly anti-social.

Fortunately, specialist seed merchants can supply wild flower seeds, so there is no reason why you should not grow your own if you want to make violet syrup or cowslip wine.

It is best to pick flowers on a dry day, and in the early part of the day, after the dew has dried but before the sun is hot enough to evaporate the essential oils. Choose fully open specimens, undamaged by insects or disease. Shake them to remove any tiny insects. Use your judgement as to whether or not the flowers should be rinsed. If so, do it quickly in ice-cold water, and lay the flowers to dry on two or three layers of paper towels before proceeding with the recipe. It is best to use the flowers within a few hours of picking, but if you do need to store them for a day or two, surround them with a damp – not wet – tea-towel and seal them in an airtight box in the refrigerator.

To dry flower petals

Place the petals in a single layer on a foil-lined baking sheet and put this in the oven set at 100°C/200°F/gas mark ¼ for about 2 hours or until the petals are dry enough to crumble. Store them in an airtight jar in a cool, dark place and use them as you would other herbs, within 12 months, until the flowers are in bloom again.

Protected species

English Nature (www.english-nature.org.uk) and the Joint Nature Conservation Committee (www.jncc.org.uk) are among the best sources of guidance, highlighting the different pieces of legislation that protect certain flowers, and also the European Directives dealing with the same subject.

Food colouring

Occasionally – and sparingly – I use food colouring to add a subtle tint to a lavender butter cream, for example, or to the Battenberg cake mix. The best range of colourings I have found is the Queen's brand from Australia, which comes in a box with four small (7 ml) plastic vials, including yellow, green, pink and purple, together with a chart which shows you how to mix to obtain other colours. The pink and purple are very soft indeed, and the green is more natural-looking than the viridian green so often found.

Making your own

There are some floral components to recipes, however, that you might want to make yourself because they keep well. For example, flower sugars can be kept in airtight containers in a cool, dark place. And, just as it is useful to keep a jar of red-currant jelly in the cupboard for glazing tarts, you will probably want to make several jars of rose petal jelly and lavender jelly for your floral baking so you can use these scents and flavours throughout the year and not just during the flower season.

Whilst crystallised flowers and flower petals are available commercially, in my experience they are increasingly hard to find, and very expensive, especially roses and violets.

It isn't difficult to crystallise flowers at home and doesn't require a large number of ingredients or complicated equipment. However, it is delicate work, requiring patience and a little manual dexterity. All you need is a fine-tipped artist's paintbrush, a small fine sieve, a wire rack and baking parchment. Fine tweezers are also useful.

I recommend small flowers such as violets, rose petals, jasmine flowers, lilac flowers, mimosa, borage flowers and lavender buds for crystallising; all should be freshly picked on a sunny day after the dew has dried.

There are two ways of crystallising flowers, one using egg white and one using gum tragacanth. Also known as powdered tragacanth or gum Arabic, this is used for preserving and frosting flower petals. It is no longer widely available, usually only on order through independent high-street pharmacies.

Crystallised flowers

Both these recipes are sufficient for about 40 to 60 small flowers or rose petals, but it is not a good idea to pick so many at once, as they will wilt. Pick and work with a few at a time for the best results.

Method 1

Cover a wire rack with baking parchment.

Whisk the egg white to a light foam, adding the spirit at the end. This helps the egg white and sugar to dry and therefore set more quickly. Hold the flower or petal at the base and paint it all over with the egg white, top and underside, taking care to include all edges and folds between the petals. Using the sieve or your fingers, gently sprinkle on the sugar, ensuring that the flower is well coated but not clogged with sugar. Place the flower on the wire rack. When you have crystallised all the flowers, put them in a cool, well-ventilated place to dry completely, when they will feel stiff and be very brittle. Carefully store them in airtight boxes lined with baking parchment and layered between sheets of parchment.

1 egg white
½ teaspoon high-proof grappa or vodka
100 g / 3 ½ oz / scant ½ cup caster sugar

Method 2

Cover a wire rack with baking parchment.

Mix the gum tragacanth and water, then paint it on the flower and proceed as described above.

1 tablespoon gum tragacanth
3 tablespoons water
100 g / 3 ½ oz / scant ½ cup caster sugar

Rose petal sugar

Use the deepest pink or red rose petals, from
old-fashioned scented varieties, such as *Rosa
officinalis*, the apothecary's rose, *R. gallica*,
R. damascena and *R. centifolia*. The wild rose,
Rosa rugosa, is also suitable as it is richly
scented, with a beautiful deep purple red, not
to be confused with the other wild rose, the
pale dog rose, *Rosa canina*.

Spread freshly gathered rose petals in a single
layer on a clean tea towel or paper towel and
leave to dry for up to 12 hours, depending on
the humidity of the room in which you are
working, most likely the kitchen, as few of us
have still-rooms these days. Put the petals in a
food-processor with the sugar and process until
the mixture is well blended. Unless you want
the sugar for immediate use, it is important
that the flowers are dry before you grind
them, otherwise your food-processor will be
a mass of sugar paste before you know what
has happened. To be on the safe side, once the
flowers are ground, spread the sugar out on
a sheet of baking parchment and, as it dries,
break up any clumps that form before pouring
the sugar into jars for storing.

Lavender sugar

When making lavender sugar, you need to
choose lavender (*L. augustifolia*, Hidcote) in
full bloom and pick off each individual flower
with a pair of tweezers for the purest colour. If
you simply separate from the stalk the flowers
enclosed in the sepals, you will get a greenish
sugar.

Take freshly picked lavender and allow it to dry out for an hour or two. Then grind with preserving or granulated sugar. About 10 parts sugar to 1 part flowers is usually about right, but this needs to be tested, as the concentration of fragrant oils varies according to the amount of sun. Once you have ground the sugar, spread it out on greaseproof paper to dry further and, as it dries, break up the clumps which may have formed if the flowers were at all damp. I usually also add a couple of whole sprigs of lavender to the jar. Alternatively, simply layer sugar in a large jar with lavender heads. Over time some buds will detach themselves from the stalk and you will probably want to sift some of them out of the sugar before using.

Store the sugar in an airtight container in a dark, dry place. This is best used within a year. Much longer than that and the lavender flavour changes from floral and subtle to something spicy, almost akin to ginger. I have found this particularly noticeable when making lavender shortbread with year-old lavender sugar rather than freshly ground sugar.

Lavender jelly

Wash the apples, cut them into chunks and put in a large saucepan. Cover with water and simmer until the apples are soft. Strain the pulp through a jelly bag without squeezing or forcing; otherwise, the jelly will be cloudy.

Measure the liquid and add 450 g/1 lb/2 cups sugar for each 600 ml/20 fl oz/2½ cups of liquid. Strain the lemon juice into a saucepan, and add the apple extract and sugar, together

makes about 2 kg/4 lb

10 medium-size tart apples
  – Granny Smiths are very
  good, as are most cooking
  apples
10 to 15 sprigs of lavender
juice of 2 lemons
granulated or preserving
  sugar – see recipe

with 5 of the lavender sprigs tied in muslin, or secured in a tea filter. Bring to the boil, and boil fast for 10 minutes or until setting point is reached, which is when a drop of syrup will set on a cold saucer.

Remove the lavender and pour the jelly into sterilised jars. Add an extra sprig of lavender to each jar for identification, seal and label.

Jasmine jelly

Put the fresh flowers in a saucepan. Pour on the boiling water to cover them, let it come back to the boil and simmer for 5 minutes. Remove from the heat and let the flowers steep for several hours, or overnight if you wish.

Put a fine cloth, muslin or lawn, in a sieve and ladle in the liquid and flowers. Press down to extract as much liquid as possible, then discard the flowers. Pour the lime juice through a sieve into a measuring jug and add the jasmine water extract, bringing the liquid up to 500 ml/ 18 fl oz/2 cups. Pour the liquid and sugar into a heavy saucepan, stirring in the tartaric acid. Heat gently until the sugar has dissolved, then bring to the boil and, once boiling, keep at a fierce boil for 4 minutes, by which time the mixture should 'jell'. Pour into hot jars, seal, label and store in a dark place, to keep the jelly nice and pale.

makes three 250 g/ 8 oz jars

75 g/3 oz/1 cup jasmine flowers
600 ml/20 fl oz/2½ cups water
juice of 2 limes
½ teaspoon tartaric acid
450 g/1 lb/2 cups jam sugar (with added pectin)

Cook's note

Use the same recipe and method to make jellies of rose petal, clove carnation and elderflower, substituting lemon for lime. In the unlikely event that you might gather sufficient violets, you can follow the recipe and method to make violet jelly.

Rose petal syrup

This easily made syrup can be used to flavour all manner of creams, custards, ice-creams and sorbets. Clove carnations, elderflowers, jasmine and violets can be used in the same way. If making lavender syrup, use 1 tablespoon of lavender flowers only, as they are much stronger in flavour than the other flowers.

Boil the water, pour it over the flower petals and leave overnight. Then put all the ingredients in a saucepan and heat gently until the sugar has dissolved. Bring to the boil, simmer for 2 or 3 minutes before removing from the heat and leave until cold. Strain, bottle and label.

makes 600 ml/20 fl oz

400 ml/14 fl oz/1¾ cups
water
50 g/2 oz rose petals
400 g/14 oz/2 cups
granulated sugar

Floral butter cream

For filling sponge cakes, for topping cup cakes, for garnishing delicate teatime fancies, for sandwiching macaroons and meringues, floral butter cream has a number of uses, and is very easy to make. It can also be frozen, as you would ordinary butter, because it contains very little liquid.

Gently mix the butter and sugar together and gradually add the floral water or essence, and food colouring if using it. Use immediately or chill until required, and then allow to return to room temperature for spreading.

**makes 225 g/9 oz/
1½ cups**

175 g/6 oz/1½ sticks
unsalted butter, softened
75 g/3 oz/⅔ cup icing sugar
1 tablespoon flower water *or*
a few drops of your chosen
floral essence
a drop or two of food
colouring – optional

Floral pastry cream

Use this to fill éclairs and other choux pastry buns.

Bring the milk to the boil in a saucepan and beat in the sugar, cornstarch and eggs. Put the saucepan back on medium heat while stirring constantly with a wire whisk until the custard starts to thicken. Remove from the heat, whisk once more and allow to cool. When the custard is almost cold, stir in the floral water or essence. Whip the cream and carefully fold it into the custard with a palette knife. Cover and keep in the fridge until ready to use.

**makes about 500 ml/
16 fl oz/2 cups**

225 ml/8 fl oz/1 cup milk
1 egg and 2 extra yolks,
   lightly beaten
50 g/2 oz/¼ cup caster
   sugar
25 g/1 oz/3 tablespoons
   cornflour
50 ml/2 fl oz/¼ cup double
   cream
4 tablespoons flower water *or*
   a few drops floral essence
   to taste

Floral glacé or water icing

Mix 6 parts sugar and 1 part lemon juice to the required texture, add the colouring – if using it – and the floral essence. I have experimented making the icing with, for example, rosewater instead of lemon juice, and omitting the rose essence, but it makes for too sweet an icing.

icing sugar, sifted
lemon juice, strained
a drop of food colouring –
   optional
a drop or two of culinary floral
   essence

Temperatures, equipment and ingredients

Baking temperature

The oven should **always** be preheated before baking.

Rough puff pastry and flaky pastry require a hot oven: 200–230°C/425–450°F/gas mark 7–8.

Scones, short crust pastry, buns and small cakes require a moderately hot oven: 190–200°C/375–400°F/gas mark 5–6.

Medium-size cakes such as a Victoria sandwich require a moderate oven: 160–180°C/325–350°F/gas mark 3–4.

Large cakes, such as rich fruit cakes, need a moderate heat for the first half of baking, then a slow oven to finish them at 130–150°C/275–300°F/gas mark 1–2. And do not open the oven door for the first 30 minutes. Open and close the oven door gently, avoiding draughts and vibration which may cause the cake to sink. Thoroughly grease and flour any cake tins before using them. If you use a particularly rich mix, full of fruit and sugar, as for a Christmas cake, it is a good idea to line the tin first with several thicknesses of baking parchment.

Equipment

If you are thinking about upgrading your baking equipment, a browse through the websites of stockists of baking equipment or a walk through the kitchenware section of any department store will reveal items you did not even know you could not do without. A tray of dimple cake moulds? How perfect. With these you can bake small cakes which, when turned out, have a depression in the middle that you can fill with floral butter cream or rose petal jelly. But you will also find scalloped moulds, fluted squares, hearts, miniature Bundt pans and many more, all in convenient trays of 6 or 12.

My previous clear-out of my baking cupboard was at the time

when Silpat was the new big thing in baking. Now silicone has revolutionised baking equipment far beyond this useful flexible non-stick baking sheet and there is almost nothing you cannot bake in silicone if you want to get rid of rattling bun tins and noisy racks of cake tins.

A mixer or a food-processor? Both have their fans, especially for large-scale baking. On the whole, I prefer to mix by hand, as this gives a better feel of how the ingredients are interacting. I was once making savoury scones for a large event and was persuaded to use the food-processor; the end result was heavy because I had over-mixed the dry and wet ingredients. Now, if I am baking large quantities of scones, say for a charity tea, or a week of traditional English afternoon tea in a New York hotel, I will use the food-processor to quickly blend the flour and butter, which I then store in an airtight container in the fridge until ready to use. Then I simply take out as much of the dry mix as I need and add the liquid by hand. Otherwise, for quantities up to one kilo of flour, I mix it all by hand. However, a hand-held electric beater makes light work of creaming butter and sugar and whisking egg whites.

What kind of mixing bowl? Apart from the Christmas cake and other dense fruitcakes, for which I use a large stoneware bowl, I like to use a tough but lightweight plastic jug with a handle, holding about 2 litres. There is almost nothing I cannot mix in this, from scones, to pastry to sponge cakes.

What about scales? Baking requires a good deal of accuracy in order to combine the flour/sugar/butter/eggs in the right proportions, so a well-calibrated electronic scale would be the equipment of choice, if you have the space for it.

A wire or coated rack on which to cool turned-out cakes and tarts is essential if they are not to have a soggy bottom.

The duo of spatula and wooden spoon I find essential when making light sponge cakes by hand, the spatula for folding in the flour and the wooden spoon for beating in the eggs. These operations are best done separately and alternately, so that the eggs do not curdle when adding them all at once and so that the flour does not go lumpy, which happens if you try to mix it in with the egg.

A flour sifter is useful for flouring your worktop before rolling out pastry, but a fine sieve will do the job just as well.

Baking parchment for lining cake tins and baking sheets is invaluable, and as it has so many other uses in the kitchen – cooking fish *en papillote* for example – I always keep a roll or two.

Loaf tins do not come in standard sizes. I have three which purport to be 1 kilo tins, but each has different dimensions. When choosing which one to use, add up the approximate weight of ingredients in the recipe and transpose that into volume. Measure the same volume of water into a jug and pour it into your loaf tin. Ideally, the liquid should come to within no more than 2 to 3 centimetres (about 1 inch) of the rim, to allow for the cake to rise. *Home Measures* by Shirley Bond is an extremely useful reference to sizes and measurements in the kitchen, as well as the home more generally.

Having said all that about equipment, some of my best baking has been done with the most basic equipment. Moving house into a new but poorly equipped kitchen, one of the first things I wanted to do was bake, so had to use what was to hand. The most important piece of kit was a clean 150 gram yoghurt pot which I used for measuring out the flour and sugar. Knowing that a medium egg weighs about 55 grams, I felt safe cracking 3 eggs. As for the butter, most packs are now helpfully marked in 50 gram sections; and had I been baking in America I would have known that 1 stick of butter weighs 4 ounces or 112 grams to be precise, so 1⅓ sticks would have given me the right quantity of butter. So there I had my 'pound cake', which I mixed in a saucepan and baked in an old aluminium ice cube tray without the plastic dividers. I could not have baked a better cake with all the fancy kit in the world.

Ingredients

Flour, fat, sugar and eggs are the basic ingredients for baking.

Eggs – I use organic eggs in all my cooking, so use these when baking too.

Sugar – fine sugar such as caster sugar gives a better result for sponges and pastry. Occasionally an unrefined sugar might be called for, in which case light muscovado is a good choice. Granulated sugar and Demerara sugar are coarser and often show darker, caramelised flecks in pastry, for example.

Fat – butter is usually the fat of choice and I use both salted and unsalted, but on the whole I prefer unsalted butter for floral baking. For earlier generations, salted butter was the norm, and I never noticed any detrimental effect in my mother's baking. As an alternative to butter, or sometimes combined with it, lard is an excellent fat for baking, especially for pastry or anything which requires crispness and lightness. Olive oil is also used in baking, and in small quantities this is manageable. I find it does alter the texture of the cake if overdone, making it heavy. I prefer to use natural fats rather than margarine.

Flour – self-raising flour or plain cake flour with the addition of baking powder is used for cakes and scones and some biscuits. If self-raising flour is not available, use 20 g/4 teaspoons baking powder to 225 g/8 oz/2 cups plain flour for scones, and 15 g/1 tablespoon baking powder for 225 g/8 oz/2 cups plain flour when making sponge and other cakes.

It is important to use low-protein/low-gluten flour for cake baking or you get a very heavy cake. I learned this to my cost when baking in a New York hotel and using all-purpose flour for the cakes. I thought I would lighten the result by using extra baking powder to make the cakes rise. This, of course, did not work and a dozen sponge cakes went into the bin. What I should have done was reduce the protein/gluten content of the flour, which is what I now do. If the flour is high in protein/gluten, more than 9–10%, mix the flour with cornflour (corn starch, **not** cornmeal) in proportion 4:1, i.e.

200 g/7 oz/1¾ cups strong plain flour plus 50 g/2 oz/6 table-spoons cornflour equals 250 g/9 oz/generous 2¼ cups cake flour.

Ideally, superfine cake flour with a protein content of around 6 to 8% is the best flour to use for sponge cake.

When I use a recipe book, I do not like to be referred to another page elsewhere in the book for a 'sub-recipe' for one of the component parts. If I am making a tart, I want the pastry recipe right there alongside the filling and the garnish. If I am making éclairs, I want the choux pastry recipe to hand, and not to have to flip to an appendix. That is how I have constructed this book. It will inevitably lead to some repetition of methods and ingredients, but I prefer that rather than cause reader frustration.

On the other hand, for those who like to develop their own recipes, it is useful to have a brief reference section with the main basic recipes for different types of pastry, for example. These you will find at the beginning of the relevant chapter.

Quick breads and slow breads

Scones and muffins belong in the first part of this chapter, as do other baked goods that rely on soda and baking powder as the rising agent. These are the quick breads of the title, which can be made in as little as 30 minutes from first assembling your ingredients.

My 'slow breads', made with yeast, require more time to be invested, and this baking is an altogether more leisurely pursuit. But the kneading and the proving needn't be an intimidating process, especially if you make the dough work around your timetable rather than let it constrain you. There is no reason why you shouldn't let the dough prove overnight in the refrigerator. The cold will simply slow down the fermentation of the yeast, which is a good thing as this allows more flavour to develop.

Yeast breads are satisfying to make and rewarding in the end product, so do have a go. There is no need at all to make batches of loaves, with large bags of flour. Using just half a kilo of flour, one pound, you can make a substantial and appetising loaf of bread. My recipes are for hand-baking. If you have a bread–maker, simply follow the manufacturer's

"… a dessert for high summer, when strawberries are at their best and when you might have made your own rose petal syrup and sugar"

Rose and strawberry shortcake, p.35

instructions, adding my flavouring suggestions at the relevant point, usually with the last addition of liquid.

In developing your own bread recipes, simply remember the proportions of 1 teaspoon salt to approximately 225 g/8 oz/2 cups flour and approximately half liquid to flour. 450 g/1 lb/4 cups flour will make a large loaf which will bake at 180–200°C/350–400°F/gas mark 4–6 for about 50 minutes. The same quantity will make 12 to 18 bread rolls; these will bake at the same temperature in about 15 to 20 minutes.

Try mixing wholemeal and white flour for a different loaf, and experiment with additions of other grains and seeds, such as sunflower and sesame. If you make an entirely wholemeal loaf, you'll find you need to add a little more water. Marigold petals and fennel flowers are also good in bread, and you might want to add a little grated cheese for a savoury loaf.

Two basic quick bread recipes

Scones

A trick she had learned from her mother-in-law, my mother taught me to put the scones close together on the baking sheet to encourage them to rise well and evenly. It never fails, and gives a nice tender edge to the scone, which is important as scones are meant to be split open with the fingers, not cut with a knife.

Cut out the scones with a sharp cutter, as a blunt one will compress the edges so that you will not get the light flaky effect. For the same

makes 10 to 12

225 g/8 oz/2 cups self-raising flour
50 g/2 oz/½ stick butter, chilled and diced
1 tablespoon golden caster sugar
150 ml/5 fl oz/⅔ cup soured milk, buttermilk or yoghurt mixed with water

reason, do not twist the cutter as you press it into the dough.

Using your fingertips, rub the flour and butter together until they resemble coarse bread-crumbs. Stir in the sugar and enough liquid to make a soft, pliable dough. Transfer to a floured worktop and knead lightly and briefly until smooth.

Roll and cut out scones. Bake in an oven preheated to 200°C/400°F/gas mark 6 for about 15 minutes, until well-risen and golden.

Muffins

These are American-style muffins, not the English muffin, which is made with yeast. Mix the dry ingredients and then stir in the wet ingredients until just combined. The mixture remains somewhat lumpy and should not be over-mixed. Spoon into double paper cases set on a baking sheet or in greased and floured muffin tins. Bake in a preheated oven at 180°C/350°F/gas mark 4 for 15 to 20 minutes, until well-risen and golden brown.

makes 6 large or 12 small muffins

175 g/6 oz/1½ cups plain flour
2 level teaspoons baking powder
50 g/2 oz/¼ cup caster sugar
75 g/3 oz/¾ stick butter, melted
2 eggs, lightly beaten
75 ml/3 fl oz/⅓ cup milk

Saffron potato scones

These make the perfect accompaniment to a thick root-vegetable soup. Try them, too, at breakfast time with crisp bacon and a poached egg, or with hollandaise as an Egg Benedict.

Grease or line a baking sheet.

Melt the butter in a bowl and stir in the mashed potatoes and the saffron water. Then add the flour, salt and grated cheese. Roll out on a floured worktop until about 1 cm/½ inch thick, cut into rounds and place on the baking sheet. Bake in a hot oven – 250°C/475°F/gas mark 9 – for 10 to 15 minutes. Eat hot or cold, split and spread with butter, or plain. Instead of individual scones, you can also bake it in one round, marked into wedges before baking.

makes 12 to 18, depending on size

½0 g/25 saffron threads soaked in 1 tablespoon boiling water
50 g/2 oz/½ stick butter
350 g/12 oz/2 cups boiled and mashed potatoes
75 g/3 oz/¾ cup self-raising flour
a pinch of salt
75 g/3 oz/¾ cup Cheddar, grated

Marigold, olive and Manchego scones

Decorative and full of flavour, miniature versions are very good split, lightly toasted, spread with a little butter and served as an accompaniment to a summery cocktail.

Rub the flour and butter together in a bowl. Stir in the cheese, olives and marigold petals. Add enough liquid to make a soft, pliable dough. Transfer to a floured board and knead it lightly.

Roll and cut out scones. Bake at 200°C/ 400°F/gas mark 6 in a preheated oven for about 15 minutes, then leave to cool on a wire rack.

makes 12 standard or 24 miniature scones

225 g/8 oz/2 cups self-raising flour
50 g/2 oz/½ stick butter, chilled and diced
115 g/4 oz/1 cup Manchego, grated
50 g/2 oz/½ cup black or green olives, chopped
2 tablespoons fresh marigold petals
about 115 ml/4 fl oz/½ cup buttermilk *or* fresh milk soured with lemon juice

Golden fruit muffins

These are delightful served for a lazy summer brunch and, like all muffin recipes, are easy to make and quick to cook.

Grease and flour a tray of 12 muffin cups. Sift the dry ingredients, including the flowers, into a bowl. Stir in the butter or oil, eggs, the saffron and its liquid and enough butter-milk to produce a soft, quite wet mixture. Stir in the fruit and spoon the mixture into greased muffin tins, deep bun tins or paper cases arranged on a baking sheet, filling them about two-thirds full. Bake in a preheated oven at 200°C/400°C/gas mark 6 for 18 to 20 minutes. Serve warm.

makes 12

350 g/12 oz/3 cups self-raising flour

115 g/4 oz/²/₃ cup fine cornmeal

2 teaspoons baking powder

2 tablespoons golden caster sugar

a pinch of salt

1 tablespoon marigold flowers

6-8 nasturtium flowers, torn into pieces

75 g/3 oz/¾ stick unsalted butter, melted, *or* 6 tablespoons sunflower oil

2 eggs, lightly beaten

¹/₂₀ g/25 saffron threads, soaked in 1 tablespoon boiling water

225 ml/8 fl oz/1 cup buttermilk

1 tablespoon *each* chopped dried mango, apricot, peaches and gold sultanas

Apple and rose petal scones

Whilst it is hard to improve on the traditional scone recipe, this rose and apple combination is very pleasing.

Line or grease a baking sheet. Cut the butter into the flour and then rub it lightly until you have a crumb-like mixture. Stir in the apple and, if using them, the rose petals. Beat the

makes 8 to 10

115 g/4 oz/1 stick butter, chilled

350 g/12 oz/3 cups self-raising flour

1 large cooking apple, peeled and finely chopped or coarsely grated

rosewater with the egg and add to the apple and flour mixture, and mix to a stiff but elastic dough. Turn out onto a floured worktop and divide into the number of scones you need. Pat and shape the scones by hand to 2.5 cm/1 inch thick. Place on the baking sheet and bake for about 20 to 25 minutes at 200°C/400°F/gas mark 6. Once out of the oven, dredge with the sugar and serve immediately.

2 or 3 teaspoons dried rose petals, if available
1 egg
1 tablespoon rosewater
50 g/2 oz/¼ cup caster sugar

Rose and strawberry shortcake

The American shortcake, on which this is based, is nothing like Scottish shortbread, but is a quick-rising scone dough. This is a dessert for high summer, when strawberries are at their best and when you might have made your own rose petal syrup and sugar.

Put the strawberries in a bowl, sprinkle with rose petal syrup and half the sugar. Rosewater can replace the rose petal syrup, in which case you might want to increase the amount of sugar. Mash lightly with a fork.

Sift the dry ingredients together, including the rest of the sugar. Rub in the butter until it resembles coarse breadcrumbs. Beat together the yoghurt and egg, mix them in lightly and then turn out onto a floured board. Knead for half a minute and shape into a circle about 20 cm/8 inches in diameter.

Place on a baking sheet and bake in a preheated oven at 200°C/400°F/gas mark 6 for about 20 minutes, or until golden brown. Transfer to a wire rack and leave to cool.

To serve, split the cake, spread the bottom

serves 6 to 8

1 kg/2 lb strawberries, hulled and sliced
1 to 2 teaspoons rose petal syrup – see recipe
50 g/2 oz/¼ cup rose petal sugar – see p.20
225 g/8 oz/2 cups self-raising flour
a pinch of salt
75 g/3 oz/¾ stick butter, diced
3 tablespoons plain yoghurt
1 egg

to serve

unsalted butter – see recipe
225 ml/8 fl oz/1 cup whipping cream *or* whipped double cream

with butter and pile on half the strawberries. Top with the second half of shortcake. Serve the remaining strawberries separately with the cream, or pile the strawberries and whipped cream on top before serving.

Fennel flower, pancetta and Parmesan muffins

As they are non-crumbly, these muffins are very useful to serve with aperitifs.

Grease and flour a tray of 24 miniature muffin cups. Sift the dry ingredients together, stir in the fennel flowers and then add the pancetta and Parmesan. Beat the buttermilk and eggs and add them and the saffron infusion. Stir together quickly. Spoon the mixture into the prepared muffin tray or paper cases and bake in a preheated oven at 200°C/400°F/gas mark 6 for 15 to 20 minutes. Serve hot or warm.

makes 24 miniature muffins

350 g/12 oz/3 cups self-raising flour
½ teaspoon baking soda
½ teaspoon salt
1 tablespoon fennel flowers
50 g/2 oz/3 tablespoons diced pancetta, lightly fried and cooled
75 g/3 oz/¾ cup Parmesan, grated
3 eggs
225 ml/8 fl oz/1 cup buttermilk
$\frac{1}{20}$ g/25 saffron threads, soaked in 1 tablespoon boiling water
5 tablespoons melted butter, or sunflower oil

Chorizo, saffron and Manchego muffins

Here is another version, perhaps to accompany an aperitif with a Spanish flavour.

Grease and flour a tray of 24 miniature muffin cups. Sift the dry ingredients together and then stir in the cheese and chorizo. Beat

makes 24 miniature muffins

350 g/12 oz/3 cups self-raising flour
½ teaspoon baking soda
½ teaspoon salt

the eggs and the buttermilk and add them, together with the saffron infusion. Stir the wet and dry ingredients together quickly. Spoon the mixture into the prepared muffin tray or paper cases and bake in a preheated oven at 200°C/400°F/gas mark 6 for 15 to 20 minutes. Serve hot or warm.

50 g/2 oz/3 tablespoons chorizo, diced
75 g/3 oz/¾ cup Manchego, grated
3 eggs
225 ml/8 fl oz/1 cup buttermilk
1/20 g/25 saffron threads, soaked in 1 tablespoon boiling water
5 tablespoons melted butter *or* sunflower oil

Lavender, blueberry and almond muffins

These are perfect for a late summer brunch, although blueberries freeze so well that they can be enjoyed at any time of the year.

Mix the dry ingredients and stir in the wet ingredients until just combined. The mixture remains somewhat lumpy and should not be over-mixed. Spoon into double paper cases set on a baking sheet and bake in a preheated oven at 180°C/350°F/gas mark 4 for 15 to 20 minutes, until well-risen and golden brown.

makes 6 large or 12 small muffins

175 g/6 oz/1½ cups plain flour
2 tsp baking powder
50 g/2 oz/¼ cup lavender sugar – see p.20
2 tablespoons ground almonds
2–3 tablespoons fresh blueberries
75 g/3 oz/¾ stick unsalted butter, melted
1 or 2 drops culinary lavender essence
2 eggs, lightly beaten
75 ml/3 fl oz/⅓ cup milk

Yeast breads, or 'slow' breads

Basic bread recipe

Mix the dry ingredients in a bowl, make a well in the centre and pour in the liquid ingredients. Draw the flour into the centre and mix well, until the dough leaves the sides of the bowl. You can, of course, make the dough in a food-processor.

Turn onto a floured surface and knead for five minutes. Shape the dough and put it into a lightly greased 1 kg/2 lb loaf tin. Cover loosely with lightly oiled cling film and let it rise in a moderately warm place for about an hour until doubled in size.

Bake in a preheated oven at 200°C/400°F/gas mark 6 for about 50 minutes. Turn the loaf onto a wire rack and cool completely before slicing.

makes a 1 kg/2 lb loaf

450 g/1 lb/4 cups stone-ground flour
2 teaspoons salt
2 teaspoons fast-action easy-blend yeast granules
2 tablespoons olive oil
generous 300 ml/10 fl oz/ about 2 cups warm water

Saffron tea bread

This is based on the traditional Cornish saffron cake. The local treat is 'thunder and lightning' – a slice of lightly toasted saffron loaf spread with cold clotted cream, with Golden Syrup spooned on top.

Sprinkle the dried yeast on 4 tablespoons of the milk, together with 1 teaspoon of the sugar, and let it work for 10 to 15 minutes. Soak the saffron in 2 to 3 tablespoons of boiling water. Rub the fat into the flour, stir in the sugar, fruit and mixed peel. Make a well in the centre and pour in the yeast, the rosewater and the saffron liquid. Combine to a dough, adding

makes 1 loaf

2 teaspoons dried yeast
about 225 ml/8 fl oz/1 cup warm milk
50 g/2 oz/¼ cup caster sugar
1/20 g/25 saffron threads
115 g/4 oz/1 stick butter or ½ cup lard, or a mixture of the two
450 g/1 lb/4 cups strong, plain flour

more warm milk as necessary; you may need less than the quantity stated in the recipe if you are working in humid conditions, or you may need more. Knead on a floured worktop until smooth, and place in an oiled bowl. Cover with a clean, damp tea towel and let the dough rise for an hour or so in a draught-free place.

Knock the dough back by punching the air out of it. Knead it briefly on a floured worktop until smooth again then shape into a loaf. Put this in a greased and floured 1 kg/2 lb loaf tin, cover again and let the dough rise for a further 30 to 40 minutes. Bake at 180°C/350°F/gas mark 4 in a preheated oven for 50 minutes or so. The loaf can, if you wish, be brushed with an egg and milk glaze before baking.

Carefully remove the loaf from the tin and tap the base; it will sound hollow when the bread is cooked. Otherwise, return the loaf to the tin and bake for a few minutes more. When baked, remove from the tin and allow to cool on a wire rack before slicing.

115 g/4 oz/1 cup seedless raisins or sultanas, soaked for 15 minutes in Earl Grey tea
50–75 g/2–3 oz/½–¾ cup mixed candied peel
1 to 2 tablespoons rosewater

Saffron cider bread

More West Country inspiration produced this recipe, using cider as the liquid and saffron to flavour.

Sift the flour and salt into a large bowl and make a well in the centre. Cream the yeast and honey together in a jug, stir in a third of the cider and pour into the well. Gather in enough of the flour to make a thin batter without breaking the flour 'wall'. Sprinkle some of the flour over the top and let the yeast work for about 20 minutes, until the batter breaks

makes 1 loaf

1 teaspoon salt
450 g/1 lb/4 cups strong plain flour
2 teaspoons fresh yeast
2 teaspoons honey
about 225 ml/8 fl oz/1 cup dry or medium cider
1/20 g/about 25 saffron threads, soaked in 2 tablespoons boiling water

through the surface. Stir the yeast mixture into the flour, adding the rest of the cider and the soaked saffron and its liquid until you have a workable mass of dough. Turn out onto a floured worktop and knead for 15 minutes. Put the bread into an oiled bowl, cover with oiled foil or cling film and leave to rise for a couple of hours in a warm place, or let it rise slowly in the refrigerator for up to 24 hours. Turn the dough out onto a floured worktop again, punch the air out of it and give it a second kneading, but only for about 5 minutes this time. Shape into a loaf and put in a greased floured 1 kg/2 lb loaf tin or shape it into a round and place on a baking tray. Cover once more and let rise for about 45 minutes. Bake in a preheated oven at 180°C/350°F/gas mark 4 for about 50 minutes.

Carefully remove the loaf from the tin and tap the base; it will sound hollow when the bread is cooked. Otherwise, return the loaf to the pan and bake for a few minutes more. When baked, remove from the tin and allow to cool on a wire rack before slicing.

Saffron, Manchego and chorizo slipper

Made by the same method as *ciabatta*, but the flavours here owe more to Spain and its saffron harvest than to Italy. This is the perfect accompaniment to a thick vegetable soup.

Infuse the saffron in a little of the measured water, boiling. Briefly spin the flour and yeast together with the dough-blade attachment of the food-processor. With the motor on, add the oil, salt and enough water, including all the

makes 1 loaf

$^1/_{20}$ g/25 saffron threads

225 g/8 oz/2 cups strong plain flour

½ teaspoon easy blend (fast action) yeast

5 tablespoons extra virgin olive oil

½ teaspoon salt

saffron liquid, to make a firm batter or loose dough. The texture is right when it is sticky but not wet and sticks to itself rather than to your hands. Add the chorizo and cheese and process briefly until these are mixed well into the dough, then scrape the dough from the sides of the bowl. You can put the feed tube in the lid to provide a seal and leave the dough for at least 3 hours, preferably 6 or longer. I have done it this way, and it works perfectly, but I prefer to wash the food-processor bowl and get it out of the way, so I scrape the dough into a large bowl, warmed first with hot water, so as not to cool down the dough too rapidly. Cover with cling film, or put inside a large polythene bag, secured tightly closed. After 3 to 6 hours' proving, have a non-stick baking sheet or Swiss roll tray ready and gently ease the dough onto it with a rolling motion. Flouring your hands first helps. Dust the top with flour and leave to prove for 30 to 40 minutes. The dough will not rise much at this stage, but just plump out a little. Preheat the oven to 220°C/425°F/gas mark 7 and bake the loaf for about 30 minutes until golden brown and hollow-sounding. The loaf will puff up considerably while baking. Allow to cool on a wire rack before slicing.

about 200 ml/7 fl oz/⁷⁄₈ cup hand-hot water

75 g/3 oz/¾ cup chorizo, diced reasonably small

75 g/3 oz/¾ cup Manchego, grated

Nasturtium, saffron and pumpkin seed bread

The pumpkin seeds add a chewy texture, the saffron a warm, spicy fragrance and the flowers a burst of colour to this very easy and versatile bread recipe.

Soak the saffron threads in 4 tablespoons of the measured water, boiling.

makes 1 loaf

¹⁄₂₀ g/25 saffron threads

450 g/1 lb/4 cups bread flour

2 teaspoons salt

2 teaspoons fast-action easy-blend yeast

Mix the dry ingredients in a bowl, then make a well in the centre and pour in the liquid ingredients. Draw the flour into the centre and mix thoroughly, until the dough leaves the sides of the bowl. You can do all this in a mixer or food-processor if you prefer. Once the flour and liquid are combined, quickly work in the seeds and petals by hand, otherwise they will be too finely chopped.

Turn onto a floured surface and knead for five minutes. Shape the dough and put it into a lightly greased 1 kg/2 lb loaf tin. Cover loosely with lightly oiled cling film and let it rise in a moderately warm place for about an hour until it has doubled in size.

Bake in a preheated oven at 200°C/400°F/ gas mark 6 for about 35 to 40 minutes. Turn the loaf onto a wire rack and allow to cool completely before slicing.

2 tablespoons olive oil
about 300 ml/10 fl oz/
  1¼ cups warm water
75 g/3 oz/¾ cup pumpkin
  seeds
10 nasturtium flowers,
  shredded
1 tablespoon nasturtium
  seeds, chopped

Tarte tropézienne

A glass of Muscat de Beaumes de Venise is the perfect accompaniment to this rich, creamy cake from the south of France. It would be pleasing to report that this is an age-old recipe from St Tropez, but it came to the village, as it was then, with a Polish baker, Alexandre Micka, in the 1950s. He was responsible for the catering for Roger Vadim's film, *Et Dieu créa la femme* and it was Brigitte Bardot who suggested a name for the cake. Although always called a *tarte*, by which we usually mean a pastry base with a filling, it resembles a rich European *torte*, or cake, with a filling that is both pastry cream and butter cream. As the detailed recipe is secret, and also a *marque*

serves 6 to 8

Brioche dough

300 g/10 oz/2½ cups plain
  flour
1 tsp salt
2 teaspoons dried yeast
2 eggs, lightly beaten
75 g/3 oz/¾ stick butter,
  softened but not melted
50 g/2 oz/¼ cup caster
  sugar
2 tablespoons orange flower
  water
warm milk – see recipe

déposée, any recipe can only be an approximation. But the hint of orange flower water reminds us that we are in the south of France.

Put the flour, salt and dried yeast in the food-processor and pulse briefly to combine. Add the eggs, butter, sugar and orange flower water and process until well mixed and the dough leaves the side of the bowl. You may need to add a little milk during the processing to ensure enough moisture is in the dough. It should not be sloppy, but should be soft rather than firm. Turn onto a floured worktop and knead until the dough is stretchy and smooth. Gather it into a ball and place in a large greased bowl. Cover with cling film and let it prove. You can do this overnight in a relatively cool place. The dough is then ready to use.

Boil the milk with the vanilla pod and let it infuse in the saucepan for about 30 minutes. Discard the vanilla and beat in the sugar, cornflour and eggs. Put the saucepan back on medium heat while stirring constantly with a wire whisk until the custard starts to thicken. Remove from the heat and quickly whisk in the soft butter, which will cool down the custard immediately. When the custard is almost cold, stir in the orange flower water. Whip the cream and carefully fold it into the custard with a palette knife. Cover and keep in the fridge until ready to use.

Roll the prepared dough into a round and place on a greased and floured baking sheet or in a greased and floured 25 cm/10 inch sponge tin for an absolutely regular round cake. Cover with a damp cloth and let it rise for 40 minutes in a draught-free spot. Lightly brush with the glaze and sprinkle on the sugar. Bake for 25 to

Filling

250 ml/8 fl oz/1 cup milk

1 vanilla pod, split in half lengthwise

1 egg and 2 extra yolks, lightly beaten

50 g/2 oz/¼ cup caster sugar

50 g/2 oz/½ stick unsalted butter, softened

25 g/1 oz/3 tablespoons cornflour

50 ml/2 fl oz/¼ cup double cream

4 tablespoons orange flower water

To bake and assemble the cake

brioche dough – as above

1 tablespoon milk mixed with a little egg yolk – for the glaze

2 to 3 tablespoons coarse sugar

filling – as above

30 minutes at 180°C/350°F/gas mark 4 in a preheated oven. Remove from the oven once baked and transfer to a wire rack to cool.

Once cool, split the cake horizontally and fill with cream. Chill until ready to serve.

Lavender *tarte tropézienne*

Monsieur Micka, the originator of the *tarte tropézienne*, might not agree, but this recipe works beautifully with lavender and lemon. To do this, use lavender sugar (p.20) and replace the orange flower water with 2 tablespoons of grated lemon zest when making the dough. In the filling, use another 1 to 2 tablespoons of lemon zest and replace the orange flower water with a dash of culinary lavender essence (see p.14). The glass of Muscat de Beaumes de Venise goes equally well with the lavender version.

Plaited brioche

Here is another yeast bread with a Provençal flavour, which is perfect for breakfast.
Be careful if you want to toast it, however, as the sugar content browns the bread more quickly than plain bread. Any leftovers make a superior bread and butter pudding.

In a small bowl sprinkle the yeast on the warm water. In a large bowl mix the flour, salt and sugar. Stir in the liquid yeast then add the egg yolk, orange flower water and melted butter. Mix thoroughly and, when well incorporated, knead the dough for 10 minutes until it is supple and no longer sticks to your fingers. Cover the bowl and let the dough rise for an

makes 1 loaf

1 teaspoon dried yeast
115 ml/4 oz/½ cup warm water
350 g/12 oz/3 cups white bread flour
½ teaspoon salt
1 tablespoon sugar
1 whole egg and 1 egg yolk
1 tablespoon orange flower water
3 tablespoons unsalted butter, melted
1 tablespoon flaked almonds

hour. Turn out onto a floured worktop and punch out the air. Divide the dough into 3 balls, and roll each one into a rope of even size. Press the ropes together at one end and then plait them, securing the ends underneath. Place the loaf on the baking sheet and let it rise again for 30 minutes. Brush it gently with the beaten egg yolk and scatter the flaked almonds on top. Bake at 180°C/350°F/gas mark 4 for about 25 minutes, until the base sounds hollow when you tap it.

Lardy cake

This is a very traditional English farmhouse cake, from that middle belt of England where pigs have always been reared, hence the lard. Despite what you might think, lard is the perfect fat for producing light and airy baked goods.

Make a plain dough by mixing the sugar and water and sprinkling the yeast on top. When it has begun to froth, mix it with the flour and salt and 25 g/1 oz/2 tablespoons of the lard, cut into the flour. Knead until the dough is elastic and smooth. Place in an oiled bowl and cover with cling film or a damp tea towel. Let it rise until doubled in size. Knock it back and, on a floured work surface, roll it out to a rectangle 0.5 to 1 cm/¼ to ½ inch thick.

Dot the surface with a third of the lard at regular intervals and sprinkle with a third of the fruit and sugar. Sprinkle on a teaspoon of rosewater. Fold the bottom third of the dough up and the top third down so that it is folded into three. Give the dough a turn so that the short edges are at the top and bottom. Roll the

makes 16 pieces

1 teaspoon caster sugar
300 ml/10 fl oz/1¼ cups warm water
1 tablespoon dried yeast
450 g/1 lb/4 cups strong white flour
2 teaspoons salt
225 g/8 oz/1 cup lard, chilled
115 g/4 oz/1 cup mixed raisins and sultanas
115 g/4 oz/½ cup caster sugar
½ teaspoon ground nutmeg
1 tablespoon rosewater

dough out as before, dot with more lard, fruit, sugar and rosewater, fold, and turn and repeat the process once more, this time dusting on the spice with the fruit and sugar.

Roll the dough out to fit a 20 x 25 cm/8 x 10 inch greased cake tin. Score into squares or rectangles, cover with a damp tea towel or oiled cling film, and leave to prove for 20 to 30 minutes. Bake for 35 to 40 minutes, or until golden brown, at 220°C/425°F/ gas mark 7. Remove from the tin, dust with sugar and cool on a wire rack. Lardy cake is traditionally broken into pieces and not cut.

Floral Bath buns

Like the similar Sally Lunn buns, these teacakes originated in Bath in the eighteenth century, said to have been invented by Dr William Oliver, who is also credited with the Bath Oliver biscuit.

Mix the milk, yeast, eggs and 50 g/2 oz/ ½ cup of the flour in a jug and let the yeast ferment for 20 minutes or so. Rub the butter into the remaining flour, by hand, or in a food-processor, and add the sugar, the rosewater, the candied peel and most of the raisins, and then pour in the yeast mixture. Mix thoroughly and then knead until you have a soft, smooth and stretchy dough. Do not mix the peel and sultanas into the dough in the food-processor or you will be left with a sticky mass of mud-coloured dough. If you want to make the dough in the food-processor, add the peel and sultanas by hand when you are kneading.

makes 12

150 ml/5 fl oz/¾ cup warm milk

2 teaspoons dried yeast

4 eggs

450 g/1 lb/4 cups plain flour

225 g/8 oz/2 sticks butter

150 g/5 oz/²/₃ cup golden caster sugar

2 tablespoons rosewater, plus extra for glazing

50 g/2 oz/½ cup candied orange peel, finely chopped

50 g/2 oz/½ cup sultanas

coarse sugar such as preserving sugar

Self Service Receipt for Check Out

Name: **********3495

Title: Mrs Dalloway / [paperback]

Item: 30129068902221

Due Back: 18/02/2022

Title: Wonderland : a year of
Britain's wildlife, day by day

Item: 30129086230225

Due Back: 18/02/2022

Total Check Out: 2
28/01/2022 16:49:24

Cover the dough and let it rise until doubled in volume. Knock it back, and shape into buns. Place on a greased baking sheet, brush with rosewater or egg and sprinkle on the rest of the raisins and plenty of coarse sugar.

Let the buns rise for 15 to 20 minutes then bake in a preheated oven at 200°C/400°F/ gas mark 6 for 20 to 25 minutes. Cool on wire racks.

York Mayne bread

This is a treasure I found in my mother's Yorkshire Women's Institute Recipe Book, dating from about 1955. York Mayne Bread was recorded as early as 1445, when it was the custom to present it to important visitors to the city, a practice that continued until the latter half of the seventeenth century, after which the recipe seemed to be lost and the bread fell out of fashion as spiced bread became more popular. But intensive research in 1950 unearthed the recipe, and samples of it were made and given to guests at the York Festival in 1951. The use of rosewater, which is faithful to the original recipe, and not my own adaptation, certainly points to the recipe's early origins. I have even included caraway seeds in the interests of authenticity, even though I cannot bear them, and when I make the tea bread at home I use extra coriander seeds, which I like.

Mix the flour, sugar and spices together in a large mixing bowl. In a small bowl beat the eggs, rose essence and rosewater. In another bowl whisk the egg whites until stiff. In a third small bowl mix the yeast and warm liquid.

makes 12 to 15 pieces

350 g/12 oz/3 cups plain flour

225 g/8 oz/1 cup caster sugar

1 generous teaspoon caraway seeds

1 generous teaspoon coriander seeds

3 egg yolks

a drop or two of rose culinary essence

1 tablespoon rosewater

2 egg whites

½ oz fresh yeast *or* 1 teaspoon dried yeast

about 75 ml/3 oz/⅔ cup warm skimmed milk, *or* water and whole milk mixed

Let this begin to work and froth and, when it does so, add it and the egg mixture to the dry ingredients, mixing well, then fold in the whisked egg whites. Cover with a damp cloth and leave to rise in a warm place for 20 to 30 minutes. Turn the dough out onto a floured worktop, roll out and cut into shapes, lozenges or rounds as the fancy takes you – medieval recipes are notoriously short of detail! – and leave to rise in a warm place for another 10 minutes. Bake at 180°C/350°F/gas mark 4 for about 15 minutes until golden brown. Cool on a wire rack. Split and serve buttered with jam, or eat plain.

Tea loaves and fruit cakes

A decent afternoon tea can easily spoil one's appetite for supper, but from time to time this is a sacrifice well worth making. Amongst my own indispensable teatime treats, including small but generously filled sandwiches, warm scones and home-made preserves and dainty pastries, there will always be a tea loaf or a fruit cake. Moist yet substantial, these are big cakes, designed to be eaten after the scones and sandwiches, and before the sponge cakes and the dainties.

Because of their sturdy quality, these are perfect cakes for picnics and outdoor teas, as well as for hampers. As a thoughtful gift, you might want to consider making up an afternoon-tea hamper of home-made produce. Include a pot or two of jam, a fruit cake or tea loaf, some shortbread, a jar of clotted cream – if for fairly immediate consumption – and a cellophane packet of home-made scone mixture, together with a recipe and instructions for use. A pretty teapot and packet of single-estate tea complete the gift.

Mrs Beeton wrote at length about the joys of afternoon tea and the merits of high tea, and

"This is an excellent fruit cake for summer, using the lighter Mediterranean and tropical fruits, rather than dark vine fruits … the kind that would have been taken on picnics with 'lashings of ginger beer'."

Tennis cake, p.50

has a menu for an afternoon tea served as a buffet for forty guests; sandwich fillings are sardine, cucumber, *foie gras*, caviare, anchovy and salad. There are the large cakes – a Genoa, a Victoria sandwich, an almond sponge and a Madeira cake. Small cakes include castle cakes, macaroons and Piccolomini cakes, which are sponge cakes flavoured with rosewater and nutmeg. Beverages offered are not just tea, but coffee, champagne cup, claret cup, port and sherry, and there are platters of strawberries, cherries and grapes. It is actually hard to fault Mrs Beeton on menus. The tennis cake recipe that follows is based on one of Mrs B's.

Tennis cake

This is an excellent fruit cake for summer, using the lighter Mediterranean and tropical fruits, rather than dark vine fruits. A sturdy cake, this is the kind that would have been taken on picnics with 'lashings of ginger beer'.

Pour half the spirit over the fruit, nuts and ginger, and let it soak while you prepare the cake batter. Cream the butter and sugar, then add the eggs and flour alternately, together with the salt. When thoroughly mixed, stir in the soaked fruit and add enough milk to give a soft dropping consistency to the mixture. Grease and line a 20 cm/8 inch square or a 23 cm/9 inch round cake tin, and spoon in the mixture.

Smooth the top, and bake for about 2½ to 3 hours in a preheated oven at 160°C/325°F/gas mark 3 or until a skewer pushed into the centre emerges clean. Allow to cool in the tin.

serves 10 to 12

6 tablespoons white rum
115 g/4 oz/1 cup *each*
    dried peaches, apricots,
    cherries, mango,
    pineapple, sultanas and
    chopped mixed citrus peel,
    un-dyed
225 g/8 oz/2 cups blanched
    almonds, chopped
1 tablespoon crystallised
    ginger, finely chopped
1–2 teaspoons freshly grated
    ginger
225 g/8 oz/2 sticks unsalted
    butter
115 g/4 oz/½ cup caster
    sugar
115 g/4 oz/½ cup lavender
    sugar – see p.20

Pour the remaining spirit over the cake, having poked holes in it with a skewer.

Cover the cake with foil and allow to stand in a cool place until the spirit is absorbed. Then wrap the cake in greaseproof paper and foil. It will keep for several weeks, but is also extremely good as soon as it is completely cold. If I want to serve it immediately, I leave out the last slug of spirit, otherwise the alcohol does not have time to evaporate and it rather overpowers the delicious fruitiness of the cake. This freezes well.

4 eggs, lightly beaten
350 g/12 oz/3 cups self-raising flour
a pinch of salt
milk – see recipe

Sloe gin cake

Here is another excellent fruit cake, rich with the flavour of that quintessentially English liqueur, sloe gin, combined with the fragrance of rose petals.

Line a 1 kg/2 lb loaf tin. Cream the butter and sugar until light and fluffy. Lightly beat the rosewater and eggs, beat them into the butter and sugar mixture and fold in the flour alternately. Stir in the rest of the ingredients, adding enough milk to give a soft dropping consistency to the mixture. Spoon the mixture into the prepared loaf tin, smooth the top and bake for 2 to 2 ½ hours in a preheated oven at 160°C/325°F/gas mark 3 or until a skewer pushed into the centre emerges clean. Allow to cool in the tin. Remove then wrap the cake in greaseproof paper and foil. It will keep for several weeks. This freezes well.

serves 8 to 10

225 g/8 oz/2 sticks unsalted butter
115 g/4 oz/½ cup light muscovado sugar
115 g/4 oz/½ cup rose petal sugar – see p.20
4 eggs
1–2 tablespoons rosewater
250 g/9 oz/2¼ cups self-raising flour
a pinch of salt
115 g/4 oz/1 cup walnuts, chopped
115 g/4 oz/1 cup un-dyed glacé cherries
150 g/6 oz/1 cup pitted prunes, chopped
75 ml/3 fl oz/6 tablespoons sloe gin
milk – see recipe

Saffron, date and walnut loaf

This moist loaf keeps well, so I always make two, in a couple of 500 g/1 lb loaf tins. Grease and flour the tins and line their bottoms with baking parchment.

Cream the butter until soft and then beat in the sugar. Work together for a few minutes until the mixture is light and creamy. Sift the flours, spices, baking powder and salt together. Sprinkle a good tablespoon or so of the flour over the dates and mix them and the walnuts into the cake batter. Beat the eggs and stir them into the mixture, together with the saffron liquid, a little at a time, alternating with folding in the remaining flour.

Add the milk and mix thoroughly. Fill the loaf tins with the cake batter and smooth the surface. Bake for 1 to 1¼ hours at 180°C/350°F/gas mark 4. When cooked, a knifepoint or skewer inserted into the centre of the loaves will come out clean.

Remove the tins from the oven. Leave them to rest for 5 minutes and then turn the loaves out to cool on a wire rack. Peel off the greaseproof paper while still warm.

makes 2 loaves

⅟₂₀ g/25 saffron threads soaked in 2 tablespoons boiling water
175 g/6 oz/1½ sticks unsalted butter, plus extra for greasing
175 g/6 oz/¾ cup light muscovado sugar
225 g/8 oz/2 cups plain flour
225 g/8 oz/2 cups self-raising flour
½ teaspoon salt
2 teaspoons ground allspice
2 teaspoons ground nutmeg
1 teaspoon powdered cinnamon
1½ teaspoons baking powder
225 g/8 oz/2 cups stoned and chopped dates
225 g/8 oz/2 cups chopped walnuts
3 eggs
about 150 ml/5 fl oz/⅔ cup milk

Pistachio, date and orange flower tea loaf

These tea loaves keep well, once wrapped and stored, and they also freeze well. You can prepare the dates the night before baking.

Grease and flour two loaf tins. Place the dates in a bowl, mix the bicarbonate of soda with the boiling water, pour it over the dates and leave until cold. Cream the butter and sugar and add the beaten eggs, alternating with some of the flour. Gradually fold in the rest of the flour, adding the liquid in which the dates soaked, as well as the orange zest and juice, the orange flower water, the dates and the nuts. Mix thoroughly and spoon into the loaf tins. Bake at 180°C/350°F/gas mark 4 for about 1¼ hours, checking with a skewer.

Cool in the tins for 10 minutes, then on a wire rack. Serve sliced and buttered or plain.

makes 2 loaves

1½ teaspoons bicarbonate of soda
150 ml/5 fl oz/⁵⁄₈ cup boiling water
450 g/1 lb/4 cups stoned and chopped dates
50 g/2 oz/½ stick unsalted butter
350 g/12 oz/1½ cups caster sugar
2 eggs
450 g/1 lb/4 cups self-raising flour
zest and juice of 1 large orange
3 tablespoons orange flower water
75 g/3 oz/¾ cup peeled, chopped and blanched pistachios

Pain d'épices – spiced orange loaf

As well as making an excellent tea loaf, the cake can be sliced very thinly and the slices crisped in the oven, almost as for Melba toast, and then served with chicken liver mousse or terrine of *foie gras*. Crisped in this fashion it also makes an excellent garnish for desserts such as poached pears or fruit compote.

Cream the butter and sugar, and gradually add the eggs. Mix the flour and the dry ingredients, and into this gradually beat the juice and

serves 6 to 8

115 g/4 oz/1 stick unsalted butter, softened
225 g/8 oz/1 cup Demerara or light muscovado sugar
3 eggs, lightly beaten
225 g/8 oz/2 cups self-raising flour
1 tablespoon ground almonds
1 teaspoon *each* ground cinnamon, ginger,

mandarin zest, the orange flower water and the milk, as well as the marmalade. Fold the two mixtures together until thoroughly incorporated, and pour into a lined and greased loaf tin (1½–2 lb/750–1 kg). Bake for an hour in a preheated oven at 180°C/350°F/gas mark 4.

cardamon and cloves
juice and zest of 1 mandarin
2 tablespoons orange flower water
about 6 tablespoons milk
2 tablespoons fine cut or chopped orange marmalade

Jasmine tea and apricot loaf

Macerate the dried apricots in the tea and leave overnight. Cream the sugar and butter, then beat in the eggs, one at a time, alternating with flour, which you fold in. Add the drained macerated apricots and the juice and zest from the citrus fruit. Spoon the loose batter into a lined and greased 1 kg/2 lb loaf tin and bake in preheated oven at 180°C/350°F/gas mark 4 for 1 to 1¼ hours or until a skewer comes out clean. Cool in the tin for 10 minutes then remove and place on a wire rack. Heat the honey and brush over the cake. When cool, serve the cake thinly sliced. This keeps well in an airtight tin for a week.

serves 6 to 8

300 g/10 oz/2½ cups dried apricots, chopped
300 ml/10 fl oz/1¼ cups hot, brewed jasmine tea made with 1 teaspoon of jasmine tea and 2 teaspoons dried jasmine
115 g/4 oz/½ cup caster sugar
115 g/4 oz/1 stick unsalted butter, softened
3 eggs
225 g/8 oz/2 cups self-raising flour
juice and zest of 1 orange
juice and zest of 1 lemon
2 tablespoons honey

Orange tea loaf

This is a simple treat for afternoon tea and is an easy recipe to adapt to other flavours. For example, take out a quarter of the cake batter, mix it with coffee essence and a coffee liqueur, then swirl it lightly back into the batter as you spoon it into the loaf tin; this will give you a marbled coffee and orange cake. A chocolate and orange one can be made in the same way. Alternatively, add a handful or two of chopped crystallised lemon peel and some grated zest, or some ground ginger and chopped crystallised ginger. It is particularly good made with Seville oranges.

Beat the egg yolks and sugar until pale and creamy. Add the orange juice and zest, butter and a quarter of the flour, mixing well. Fold in the rest of the flour and the orange flower water then the stiffly whisked egg whites. Spoon into a greased and floured loaf tin and bake for about 45 minutes at 180°C/350°F/gas mark 4 or until a skewer inserted in the middle comes out clean.

serves 6 to 8

4 large eggs, separated
175 g/6 oz/¾ cup golden caster sugar
juice and zest of 1 bitter orange
225 g/8 oz/2 sticks unsalted butter, softened
225 g/8 oz/2 cups self-raising flour
1 tablespoon orange flower water

Blueberry, lavender and hazelnut loaf, with cinnamon lavender crunch topping

Blend the first four ingredients to a smooth batter. Grind the hazelnuts, but not too fine, and keep back about 1½ tablespoons. Stir the nuts and blueberries into the cake mix and spoon into a 1 kg/2 lb loaf tin lined with baking parchment. Make a depression down the centre with the back of the spoon. Mix together reserved hazelnuts, lavender sugar and cinnamon and sprinkle on the surface of the cake. Bake for about 45 minutes in a preheated oven at 180°C/350°F/gas mark 4, or until a skewer inserted the middle comes out clean.

Remove from the oven, cool in the tin for 5 minutes, then lift out by holding the baking parchment and allow to cool completely on a wire rack.

serves 4 to 6

115 g/4 oz/1 stick unsalted butter, softened
50 g/2 oz/¼ cup lavender sugar plus 2 tablespoons for topping – see p.20
50 g/2 oz/¼ cup light muscovado sugar,
115 g/4 oz/1 cup self-raising flour, *mixed with*
1 teaspoon baking powder
2 eggs
115 g/4 oz/1 cup hazelnuts, chopped
115 g/4 oz/1 cup fresh blueberries
1 teaspoon ground cinnamon

Carrot and orange cake

Beat the egg yolks, sugar, orange juice and zest until you have a pale, foamy mixture. Fold in the almonds, carrots, dry ingredients and finally the orange flower water.

Whisk the egg whites to firm peaks and gently fold them into the cake mixture. Spoon into a prepared 20–25 cm/10–12 inch tin, 5 cm/2 inches high. Bake for about an hour in a preheated oven at 180°C/350°F/gas mark 4. Remove from the oven and allow to cool somewhat before removing from the tin and cooling completely.

Brush all over with sieved apricot jam, thinned with a little orange flower water, if necessary. Make a thin glaze with icing sugar and orange juice, and spread over the cake while still warm. Decorate with small marzipan carrots.

serves 10

5 eggs, separated
300 g/10 oz/1¼ cups light
    muscovado sugar
grated zest of 2 oranges
juice of 1 lemon
300 g/10 oz/1⅔ cups
    ground almonds
300 g/10 oz/2 cups finely
    grated carrot
¼ teaspoon *each*: salt,
    ground cloves, ground
    cinnamon and ground
    cardamom
2 teaspoons baking powder
75 g/3 oz/¾ cup cornflour
    or potato starch
4 tablespoons orange flower
    water
2 tablespoons sieved apricot
    jam

To decorate

orange flower water icing *or*
    sweetened cream cheese
marzipan carrots

Sponge cakes large and small

Starting with the classic Victoria sponge and some variations, this chapter will also cover the fat-less sponge, so useful when making Swiss roll-type cakes, and then smaller versions of the sponge, such as cup cakes, sponge fingers and whoopee pies.

"Gently, without squashing the tiny curls, spoon a little fairy butter into the hollow, perch the wings on top and dust with a veil of icing sugar."

Orange fairy cakes with fairy butter, p.79

Victoria sponge cake, a blueprint and some variations

This quantity makes a large cake, filling an 18 cm/7 inch round loose-based cake tin, or two shallower sponge tins, 18–19 cm/7–7½ inches in diameter.

Grease and flour the tins, or use a circle of baking parchment in the bottom and grease and flour the sides.

Cream the butter and sugar until soft and light. Add the eggs, lightly beaten, one at a time, alternating with the flour. It is best to beat the eggs in briskly, then gently fold in the flour. Don't try to mix in flour and eggs at the same

serves 8 to 10

175 g/6 oz/1½ sticks
    unsalted butter
175 g/6 oz/¾ cup caster
    sugar
175 g/6 oz/½ cups self-
    raising flour *or*
175 g/6 oz/1½ cups plain
    flour, *sifted with*
    3 scant teaspoons baking
    powder
4 eggs
1 to 2 tablespoons milk

time, as there will be more lumps, which means you will have to mix harder. To add the flour, I place a sieve over the mixing bowl and sift in a quarter at a time, if I'm using four eggs.

Once mixed, pour the cake batter into the prepared tin or tins and tap them on the work surface to make sure there are no empty spots in the tins.

Bake in the centre of the oven for approximately 55 to 60 minutes at 160°C/325°F/ gas mark 3 if in one cake tin, about 30 minutes at 180°C/350°F/gas mark 4 if in two sandwich tins, but check by inserting a skewer in the middle of the cake; when the cake is done, the skewer will emerge clean, without any batter adhering to it.

When fully baked, carefully turn the cake out onto a wire rack or several folds of clean towel and allow it to cool.

When the cake is cold, you can go to town on filling and decorating it. A very simple way to finish is to split the cake horizontally and fill with jam and whipped cream or butter cream. Place the other half on top and simply sift icing sugar over the surface.

Cassata

I like to use the Victoria sponge recipe as the base for one of my favourite cakes, the *cassata alla siciliana*. No visit to any Sicilian town or city is complete without an early halt at the nearest *pasticceria* for an espresso and a slice of *cassata*. The classic *cassata* has pale green marzipan topping, originally made with pistachios, but now invariably made with green-tinted almond paste. And the filling is creamy ricotta sweetened with chopped candied fruit and grated chocolate. It is a recipe that adapts beautifully to floral-scented baking, and I particularly like the fact that, with a ricotta filling, the cake is much less rich than with a whipped cream or butter cream filling.

A rose petal *cassata*

Put the ricotta in a bowl and flavour it with a little rosewater, a teaspoon of which can also be added to the cake batter when you add the eggs. Sweeten the ricotta, if you like, with a little sifted icing sugar and stir in the rose petals, candied peel and chocolate. A spot of red food colouring to tint the filling pink can also be added. Spread the ricotta filling on one half of the sponge and place the other on top.

I also tint the marzipan a similar pink before rolling it out to cover the cake. But before rolling out the marzipan, brush the surface of the cake with rose petal jelly, which will provide a nice sticky surface to hold the marzipan in place. Roll the marzipan into a ball, then flatten it slightly and roll out between two sheets of cling film to prevent it sticking, and carefully lay it over the cake. The glaze is simply icing sugar mixed with sieved lemon juice until you have a pouring consistency with no lumps. The trick is to cover the cake quickly with this in one go so that it dries smooth. The delicate pink marzipan will show through its veil of water icing. Crystallised rose petals (see p.19) can be used for further decoration, or shapes cut out of crystallised fruit.

serves 8 to 10

a Victoria sponge as
    described on p.57
225 g/8 oz carton ricotta
1 to 2 teaspoons rosewater
1 tablespoon crystallised rose
    petals
sifted icing sugar, to taste,
    plus extra for the glaze
2 tablespoons chopped
    candied peel
2 tablespoons coarsely grated
    chocolate, dark or white
red or pink food colouring
225 g/8 oz white marzipan
rose petal jelly – see p.20
lemon juice

An elderflower *cassata*

Make a Victoria sponge as described on p.57.
Instead of using sugar to sweeten the ricotta,
beat in some elderflower syrup. (My recipe for
elderflower syrup can be found on p.31 of *The
Scented Kitchen*, and commerical varieties are also
available.) Use the syrup to brush on the cake in
order to anchor the marzipan. Tint the marzipan
the faintest green and use fresh elderflowers
to decorate after you have glazed the cake.
This can, of course, only be done just before
serving, otherwise the flowers will discolour
unless you have the patience to crystallise them
as on p.19 with egg white and sugar.

A violet *cassata*

With a Victoria sponge as described on
p.57, I make a spring-like version of a *cassata*
decorated with crystallised violets, which
look pretty against the pale green tint of the
marzipan, and I flavour the ricotta with violet
liqueur (p.15) as well as adding crystallised
violets.

A saffron *cassata*

Proceeding in similar fashion to the rose petal
cassata, infuse a generous pinch of saffron in
2 tablespoons of boiling water and use it for
both cake and marzipan. Grate lemon zest into
the sponge mixture and use lemon juice for
the water icing.

A Valentine's *cassata*

Proceed as for the rose petal *cassata* described
on p.59, but bake the mixture in a heart-
shaped cake tin.

Rose and lavender Valentine cake

I would not usually mix two floral flavours, but I like the idea of two flavours and two colours swirled together in a floral-scented union; even better when baked in a heart-shaped tin. An alternative is to keep just one scent, rose, but colour the mixes two different shades of pink.

Butter and flour a 22 cm/9 inch cake tin.

For the first mixture, cream the butter and the sugar. Add the egg yolks and beat until light. Fold in the flour and cocoa mix.

For the second mixture, cream the butter and sugar. Fold in half the flour and all the salt, milk and rosewater. Mix thoroughly. Whisk the egg whites to firm peaks and fold into the cake mix.

Spoon large dollops of each cake mix into the prepared cake tin at random. Once the mixture is used up, draw a palette knife though it two or three times to swirl the mixture, but do not over-mix, as the pink and the chocolate should be distinct.

Bake at 180°C/350°F/gas mark 4 for 30 to 40 minutes.

Serves 6 to 8

Mix 1

50 g/2 oz/½ stick unsalted butter
115 g/4 oz/½ cup light muscovado sugar
50 g/2 oz/¼ cup lavender sugar – see p.20
4 egg yolks, *beaten with*
2 drops culinary lavender essence
175 g/6 oz/1½ cups self-raising flour, *sifted with*
3 tablespoons cocoa powder and 1 teaspoon baking powder

Mix 2

115 g/4 oz/1 stick unsalted butter
175 g/6 oz/¾ cup caster sugar
225 g/8 oz/2 cups self-raising flour
a pinch of salt
75 ml/3 fl oz/⅓ cup milk
2 tablespoons rosewater
a dash of pink or red food colouring
4 egg whites

Battenburg cake

With this recipe, I wanted to create a cake with the same flavours as the best rose and lemon Turkish Delight.

Whisk the eggs thoroughly, then add the sugar and whisk again until thick, pale and creamy. Stir in the butter alternating with the flour. Take half the mixture and colour it pink, also adding a drop or two of rose essence. Add lemon zest to the second portion.

Pour the mixture into two greased and floured 500 g/1 lb loaf tins. The mixture will fill to a depth of about 4 cm/1½ inches. Bake in a moderate oven for 15 to 20 minutes at 325–350°F/160–180°C/gas mark 3–4. Turn out and cool on a wire rack. Cut each cake down the middle, giving two yellow strips and two pink strips. Sandwich them together with lemon curd or rose petal jelly. Lightly brush the cake with the same curd or glaze and stick on the almond paste. This can be bought or made, by mixing 115 g/4 oz/⅔ cup ground almonds, 50 g/2 oz/scant ½ cup icing sugar and 50 g/2 oz/¼ cup caster sugar with enough egg white to make a stiff paste.

Traditionally the cake is marked into lozenges, scoring the top with a sharp knife.

serves 6 to 8

115 g/4 oz/1 cup self-raising flour

115 g/4 oz/½ cup caster sugar

75 g/3 oz/¾ stick unsalted butter, melted and cooled

2 eggs

culinary rose essence – see pp.14 and 15

pink colouring

lemon zest

lemon curd or rose petal jelly – see p.22

Lavender streusel cake

This is based on another family favourite; easy to make and not too rich, it is the perfect morning coffee cake.

Grease and flour a 22 cm/9 inch square tin.

serves 6 to 8

150 g/5 oz/⅔ cup caster sugar

1 tablespoon lavender sugar – see p.20

Mix the ingredients for the topping together so that it resembles chunky breadcrumbs and put to one side.

Cream the sugar and butter, beat in the eggs one at a time, alternating with the flour, which should be folded in, and adding the salt at the same time. Spoon into the prepared cake tin, flatten the top and sprinkle on the topping.

Bake for 25 to 30 minutes at 190°C/375°F/ gas mark 5. Allow to cool in the tin for a few minutes, then carefully transfer the cake to a wire rack.

75 g/3 oz/¾ stick unsalted butter
2 eggs, *lightly beaten with*
a drop of culinary lavender essence – see p.14
175 g/6 oz/1½ cups self-raising flour
a pinch of salt

Topping

50 g/2 oz/¼ cup light muscovado sugar
50 g/2 oz/¼ cup lavender sugar – see p.20
25 g/1 oz/2 tablespoons unsalted butter, melted
1 tablespoon self-raising flour
75 g/3 oz/¾ cup finely chopped almonds

Floral tray bake

The tray bake is such a useful cake recipe, and can readily be adapted to rose, violet or lavender. You can now buy a rectangular plastic box in which to keep the tray bake in its tray.

Grease and flour a tray bake tin measuring 32 x 24 cm/12 x 9 inches.

Cream the butter and sugars until soft and light. Beat in the eggs a quarter at a time, alternating with folding in the flour.

Once mixed, pour the cake batter into the prepared tin and tap it on the work surface to make sure there are no empty spots in the tin.

makes 12 pieces

200 g/7 oz/1¾ sticks butter
150 g/5 oz/⅔ cup caster sugar
50 g/2 oz/¼ cup floral sugar – see p.20
225 g/8 oz/2 cups self-raising flour
4 eggs, *lightly beaten with*
a few drops of culinary floral flavouring

Bake in the centre of the oven for 50 to 60 minutes at 160°C/325°F/gas mark 3 and check by inserting a skewer in the middle of the cake; when the cake is done, the skewer will emerge clean, without any batter adhering to it.

When fully baked, carefully turn the cake out onto a wire rack or several folds of clean towel and allow it to cool.

When the cake is cold, there are several ways of dressing it up. The simplest is to make a water ice by mixing the icing sugar, lemon juice and essence, then colour it subtly. Drizzle the icing over the cake and add crystallised flowers or petals. Another way to finish it is to split the cake horizontally and fill with jam and whipped cream or floral-flavoured butter cream. Place the other half on top and simply sift icing sugar over the surface.

Decoration

75 g/3 oz/⅔ cup icing sugar, sifted

1–2 teaspoons lemon juice

2 drops culinary floral flavouring

food colouring

crystallised flowers

Saffron cake with pears

To me, these two flavours speak of autumn, and this is a lovely cake to serve for tea, or as a pudding.

Grease and flour a 20 cm/8 inch cake tin.

Cream the butter and sugar until pale and fluffy. Gradually beat in the eggs, a little at a time, alternating with the flour and ground almonds; remember to fold in the dry ingredients, not to beat them. Add the yoghurt and the saffron liquid and mix well into the cake batter. If the mixture is still very stiff, add another spoonful of yoghurt. Spread half the mixture in the cake tin, add a generous layer of pear slices and spread the remaining cake batter on top. Scatter on the flaked

serves 6 to 8

150 g/5 oz/1¼ sticks unsalted butter, at room temperature or softer

175 g/6 oz/¾ cup caster sugar

3 eggs, lightly beaten

115 g/4 oz/1 cup plus 2 tablespoons self-raising flour

115 g/4 oz/⅔ cup ground almonds

1 tablespoon plain yoghurt

¹⁄₂₀ g/25 saffron threads soaked in 1 tablespoon boiling water

almonds and tap the tin down hard to settle them well into the surface. Bake the cake at 160°C/300°F/gas mark 3 for 30 minutes, then turn up to 180°C/350°F/gas mark 4 for 20 minutes or so. Check by poking a skewer down into the centre of the cake; it will emerge clean if the cake is baked. If not, return the cake to the oven for 3 or 4 minutes more and check again. Much will depend on how juicy the pears were.

Once baked, carefully transfer the cake to a wire rack to cool.

1 or 2 ripe pears, depending on size, peeled, cored and thinly sliced

2 or 3 tablespoons flaked almonds

Torta di mele

Signora Lancellotti in Soliera, near Modena, made us a warm apple cake for Sunday lunch one day. Instead of the grappa she used, I have included rosewater, as I like the apple and rose combination.

Butter and flour a deep cake tin; a Christmas cake tin is the very thing.

Cream the butter and sugar, and then stir in the flour and eggs alternately. Add the lemon zest. Fold in the apples and bake in a deep, well-buttered and -floured cake tin for about an hour at 180°C/350°F/gas mark 4. Carefully remove from the tin and cool on a wire rack, or serve warm.

serves 8 to 10

115 g/4 oz/½ cup caster sugar

25 g/1 oz/1 tablespoon rose petal sugar – see p.20

150 g/5 oz/1¼ cups butter

4 eggs, *lightly beaten with*

4 tablespoons rose water

350 g/12 oz/3 cups self-raising flour

zest of 1 lemon, grated

6 medium apples, peeled, quartered, cored and sliced

Marigold sponge

This is a classic Victoria sponge recipe, brightened with marigold petals and scented with a breath of orange flower water, perfect for a summer tea. You can also eat it freshly baked and still warm as a pudding, in which case I would leave out the butter cream, serve wedges of the cake dusted with icing sugar and with a scoop of clotted cream on the side.

Grease and flour two 20 cm/8 inch sandwich tins.

Grind the sugar and marigold petals in the food-processor, in which you can also do the rest of the mixing, then cream the butter and sugar thoroughly until pale, light and fluffy. Add the zest and juice, and then a little beaten egg, processing it with the butter/sugar mixture. Alternate the egg with spoonfuls of flour, blending in completely before adding the next helping of egg.

Spoon the batter into the cake tins, smooth the top and bake in a preheated oven at 180°C/350°F/gas mark 4 for 20 to 25 minutes.

Allow to cool in the tin for a few minutes and then ease the sponges out onto wire racks to cool. To serve, sandwich with a marigold butter cream and sift icing sugar over the top.

serves 6 to 8

175 g/6 oz/¾ cup granulated sugar

2 handfuls marigold petals

175 g/6 oz/1½ sticks unsalted butter, at room temperature

finely grated zest and juice of 1 orange

4 eggs, *lightly beaten with*

2 tablespoons orange flower water

175 g/6 oz/1½ cups self-raising flour, sifted

Marigold and orange butter cream

Mix the ingredients together thoroughly and, while it is still soft, spread the butter cream on one half of the sponge.

makes enough for one cake

75 g/3 oz/¾ stick unsalted butter, softened
50 g/2 oz/scant ½ cup icing sugar
1 handful marigold petals *crushed with*
1 tablespoon caster sugar
grated zest of 1 orange
1 tablespoons orange flower water

Orange flower and carrot cake

Here is a versatile recipe you can serve at teatime or warm as a pudding.

Grease and flour a sponge tin or ring mould, tube or Bundt pan.

Cream the fat and sugar until soft and creamy. Add the egg yolks and flour, alternately, and then mix in the rest of the ingredients. Whisk the egg whites, and fold into the cake mixture. Spoon the mixture into the prepared tin and bake for about 20 to 25 minutes in a preheated oven at 180°C/350°F/gas mark 4. Cool slightly in the tin before turning out. If using the syrup, bring the ingredients to the boil, allow to reduce slightly, spoon over the cake and serve hot, warm or cold with cream or custard.

If you prefer to serve this as a cake, instead of pouring a syrup over it while still warm, let the sponge cool completely before giving it a

serves 6 to 8

115 g/4 oz/1 stick unsalted butter, at room temperature
115 g/4 oz/½ cup caster sugar
3 eggs, separated, the yolks *lightly beaten with*
3 tablespoons orange flower water
115 g/4 oz/1 cup plain flour
50 g/2 oz/⅓ cup ground almonds
75 g/3 oz/½ cup finely grated carrot
finely grated zest of 1 orange

thin coating of water icing. Instead of the usual orange or lemon flavoured one, mix the juice and pulp of a passion fruit with 1 tablespoon orange flower water and then rub it through a sieve. Stir in enough sifted icing sugar to give a smooth, light spreadable consistency and use it to ice the cake.

Syrup, if serving as a pudding

6 tablespoons orange juice

4 tablespoons sugar

1 to 2 tablespoons orange flower water

Lavender, lemon and almond cake

You can make this cake quickly in a food-processor or mixer.

Line or grease and flour a 20 or 25 cm/8 or 10 inch round or square cake tin.

Cream the butter and sugar in a food-processor and then add the flour, baking powder, cream and eggs. By hand, stir the almonds and lemon peel into the cake batter, and pour into your greased floured cake tin.

Bake in a preheated oven for about 30 minutes at 180°C/350°F/gas mark 4; place no higher than the centre shelf and remove when a skewer, inserted in the middle, comes out clean.

Turn the cake out onto a rack and let it cool. Cut into squares or wedges, dust with icing sugar and serve.

serves 6 to 8

115 g/4 oz/1 stick unsalted butter, softened

50 g/2 oz/¼ cup caster sugar

50 g/2 oz/¼ cup lavender sugar – see p.20

150 g/5 oz/1¼ cups self-raising flour, *sifted with*

1 teaspoon baking powder

4 tablespoons cream

3 eggs, *beaten with*

a drop of culinary lavender essence

3 tablespoons flaked almonds

3 tablespoons chopped candied lemon peel

Triple orange and olive oil cake

This is an unusual recipe, which I baked after visiting the Cremonas for an olive-picking afternoon in Wardija, where they were making some of the first olive oil to be produced in the Maltese islands for centuries. The cake behaves like a soufflé and will sink, but don't worry as this does not spoil the flavour or texture at all.

Line a loose-bottomed 20 cm/8 inch cake tin with greaseproof paper and butter generously.

Whisk the egg yolks and sugar until pale and fluffy. Fold in the zest, orange flower water and liqueur. Beat the flour into the mixture gradually, making sure the salt is added at this stage. Add the orange juice and olive oil, ensuring that the batter is well mixed. Whisk the egg whites to firm peaks and then fold into the batter. Pour the batter into the prepared cake tin and smooth the top.

Bake in the top half of a pre-heated oven at 190°C/375°F/gas mark 5 for 20 minutes. Turn down to 160°C/325°F/gas mark 3 and bake for a further 20 minutes. Turn the heat off, cover the cake with a piece of buttered greaseproof paper to stop further browning and let the cake settle for 10 minutes. Remove from the oven and turn the cake onto a rack to cool.

serves 6 to 8

5 eggs, separated, plus 2 extra egg whites

175 g/6 oz/¾ cup caster or light muscovado sugar

grated zest of 1 orange

1 tablespoon orange flower water

1 tablespoon orange liqueur – Grand Marnier, Curaçao or Cointreau

175 g/6 oz/1½ cups self-raising flour, sifted 2 or 3 times

a good pinch of salt

75 ml/3 fl oz/⅓ cup freshly squeezed orange juice

75 ml/3 fl oz/⅓ cup olive oil

Lavender Madeira cake

Traditionally served with a glass of Madeira, hence its name, this is a good plain cake for any time, subtly enhanced with a breath of lavender.

Line a 20 cm/8 inch layer cake tin, or 1 kg/ 2 lb terrine or loaf tin, with two or three layers of greaseproof paper.

Beat the butter to a cream. Add the sugar and cream together thoroughly with the butter. Add the eggs, one at a time, alternating with a tablespoon of the flour. Beat each addition into the mixture very thoroughly before adding the

serves 8 to 10

225 g/8 oz/2 sticks unsalted butter

115 g/4 oz/½ cup lavender sugar – see p.20

115 g/4 oz/½ cup caster sugar

4 eggs

225 g/8 oz/2 cups self-raising flour

150 ml/5 fl oz/about ⅝ cup milk

next. Add the milk and the remaining flour, and incorporate this well into the mixture.

Pour the cake batter into the prepared tin and bake in a preheated oven at 180°C/350°F/gas mark 4 for 45 minutes to 1 hour.

Half-way through cooking, lay strips of lemon peel on top of the cake, return it to the oven and continue cooking for another 30 minutes, or until the cake is firm and golden brown and a skewer inserted in the centre comes out clean. Carefully turn out the cake and cool it on a wire rack. Before serving, arrange the lavender on top, 'sticking' it with a dab of jelly.

candied lemon peel
crystallised lavender buds –
    see p.19
lavender jelly – see p.21

Fatless sponge cakes

Light and airy, these sponge cakes are made without butter or other fat, and do not keep as well as the Victoria sponge, changing texture to something slightly chewy.

Mrs Hannah's sponge cake

I came across this recipe in the manuscript notebooks of the American grandmother of an old friend. Mrs Hannah would have been born in about 1860 or so in New York state. I like the recipe for its simplicity, and have adapted it to make a lavender cake. Surprisingly, because it contains no fat, this light sponge will keep for several days, and it also freezes well. The cake is also delicious served warm as a pudding with blueberries or lightly poached plums or figs.

Whisk the sugar, eggs and salt well together, and then fold in the flour, sifted with 1 teaspoon baking powder (or use self-raising

serves 6 to 8

50 g/2 oz/¼ cup lavender
    sugar
50 g/2 oz/¼ cup caster
    sugar
2 eggs
a pinch of salt
115 g/4 oz/1 cup plus
    2 tablespoons plain flour
1 teaspoon baking powder
115 ml/4 fl oz/½ cup boiling
    milk

flour). Stir in the boiling milk and pour the mixture into a tube pan. Bake for 40 to 45 minutes 'in a rather slow oven', according to Mrs Hannah's faded hand-writing; 160°C/325°F/gas mark 3 is about right. Cool in the baking tin. Slice and serve.

Orange flower roulade with dates, pistachio and ricotta

This recipe was inspired by a visit to Marrakech, where the scent of orange blossom in the gardens was so strong that it would wake me in the morning. Because this is the classic fat-less sponge mix, it is best made the day it is to be served as it does not keep well.

Line a Swiss roll tray with buttered greaseproof paper.

Whisk half the sugar and the egg yolks in a bowl set in a pan over, but not touching, simmering water until pale and foamy and the mixture leaves a ribbon when trailed on the surface.

Use a clean whisk to beat the egg whites with the remaining sugar until firm and glossy. Fold together the yolk mixture, flour and egg whites, adding the orange zest and orange flower water.

Pour the mixture into the prepared tray. Smooth the surface and bake in a preheated oven at 180°C/350°F/gas mark 4 for 12 minutes, or until the sponge begins to shrink away from the side of the tin.

Remove from the oven, turn out onto a damp

serves 6

Sponge

115 g/4 oz/½ cup caster sugar

3 eggs, separated

115 g/4 oz/1 cup plain flour, sifted

grated zest of 1 orange, mandarin or tangerine

2 tablespoons orange flower water

clean tea towel, peel off the paper, trim off the crusty edges and roll the cake while you prepare the filling.

Blend the ricotta, honey and orange flower water, and stir in the dates and pistachios. Unroll the sponge, spread with the filling and re-roll it.

Serve the same day, dusted with icing sugar.

Filling

200 g/7 oz/1¼ cup fresh ricotta

2 tablespoons orange blossom honey

2 teaspoons orange flower water

12 dates, stoned and chopped

2 to 3 tablespoons unsalted pistachios, shelled

Orange blossom roll

I have developed this recipe from one of those lovely Portuguese cakes that use many eggs and little flour, and it is very different in texture from the date and orange flower roulade on p.71. You can also make a rose version, using rose petal sugar, rosewater and a dash of pink food colouring.

Line and butter a standard Swiss roll tray.

Crack the eggs into a large bowl. Mix the dry ingredients and then add them to the eggs. Beat until pale and thick, gradually adding the orange zest and orange flower water. Pour the mixture into the prepared tin. Smooth it to the corners and bake in a preheated oven at 150°C/325°F/gas mark 3 for about 30 minutes. The mixture will seem to separate, crisp on top and translucent underneath.

Spread a sheet of greaseproof paper on a worktop and sift with icing sugar. Turn the roll out onto the sugar-covered paper, and roll it up. Place on a wire rack to cool, and then serve in small slices.

serves 8

4 large eggs

175 g/6 oz/¾ cup caster sugar

2 teaspoons flour

zest of 1 large orange, finely grated

2 to 3 teaspoons orange flower water

Lavender Swiss roll

Use lavender jelly to fill this delicate sponge roll, perfect for a summer afternoon tea. A fatless sponge, it needs to be eaten on the day it is made. A rose petal Swiss roll is equally delicious.

Line a Swiss roll tin with buttered greaseproof paper.

Whisk half the sugar and the egg yolks in a bowl set in a pan over, but *not* touching, simmering water until pale and foamy and the mixture leaves a ribbon when trailed on the surface.

Use a clean whisk to whisk the egg whites with the remaining sugar until firm and glossy. Fold together the yolk mixture, flour and egg whites, adding the lemon zest. Spoon the mixture into the prepared tin. Smooth the surface and bake in a preheated oven at 180°C/350°F/gas mark 3 for 12 minutes.

Remove from the oven, turn the cake out onto a damp clean tea towel, peel off the paper, trim off the crusty edges and roll the cake while you prepare the filling.

Whisk the cream to firm peaks. Lightly toast the almonds. Unroll the sponge. Spread on the lavender jelly and then the whipped cream. Scatter on the almonds and roll the cake again. Before serving, add a generous sifting of icing sugar to the surface.

serves 6

Sponge

50 g/2 oz/¼ cup caster sugar
50 g/2 oz/¼ cup lavender sugar – see p.20
3 eggs, separated
115 g/4 oz/1 cup plain flour, sifted
grated zest of 1 lemon

Filling

300 ml/10 fl oz/1½ cups double cream
2 tablespoons flaked almonds
lavender jelly – see p.21
icing sugar

Small sponge cakes

Rose-scented madeleines

Devoted as I am to the baking of the British Isles, I admit to feeling very proud when I made my first batch of madeleines, taught by a French pastry chef in New York, using a kilo of flour. The recipe can easily be extended, but, as you will see, a little batter goes a long way. Whilst you can make these in standard bun tins, it is worth investing in a tray of shell-shaped madeleine moulds.

Preheat the oven to 230°C/450°F/gas mark 8. Butter and flour madeleine moulds or bun tins.

Sift together the dry ingredients. Beat in the eggs and then mix in the melted butter. Pour the batter – and the mixture really is quite liquid – into the prepared moulds and bake in the top half of the oven for 5 to 7 minutes.

Remove from the oven once the madeleines are golden, well-risen and with the character-istic 'bump' in the middle.

makes 24

115 g/4 oz/½ cup rose petal sugar – see p.20
115 g/4 oz/1 cup self-raising flour
about half a coffeespoon of salt
2 eggs, lightly beaten
150 g/5 oz/1¼ sticks unsalted butter, melted

Cook's tip

I have also made orange-scented madeleines, using 2 teaspoons of orange flower water and 2 tablespoons of grated orange zest.

Lavender chocolate whoopees

Although this recipe, and the original name, sponge drops, derive from the 1950s English baking repertoire, they were made in the same way as whoopee pies, which have recently had a brief revival and, like them, were probably a way of using up left-over cake batter; the whoopee pie is said to have originated in the thrifty Amish kitchens of Pennsylvania.

Traditionally made as small, filled chocolate cakes, I have adapted the recipe to include lavender, which marries so well with chocolate.

Line or grease two baking sheets.

Whisk the sugars and egg until light and creamy. Carefully fold in the flour and cocoa mix.

Depending on the size of cake you want, place teaspoons or soupspoons of the mixture on the baking sheet well apart. Bake in a hot oven, 200°C/400°F/gas mark 6, for about 5 minutes. Transfer to wire racks to cool. When cold, sandwich with chocolate or lavender butter cream or flavoured whipped cream.

makes 8 to 12

50 g/2 oz/¼ cup caster sugar

1 tablespoon lavender sugar – see p.20

2 large eggs, *beaten with* a couple of drops of lavender culinary essence

75 g/3 oz/¾ cup self-raising flour, *sifted with*

1 to 2 tablespoons cocoa powder

Rose sponge fingers

If you leave these sponge fingers ungarnished, you can use them for trifles and charlottes.

Line or grease two baking sheets or use special moulds.

Whisk the sugars and egg until light and creamy. Carefully fold in the flour and flower petals. Pipe in fingers or fill the moulds. Bake in a hot oven, 200°C/400°F/gas mark 6, for about 5 minutes. Transfer to wire racks to cool. When cold, dip the ends of each finger in rose-scented melted chocolate and place on baking parchment to set. When the chocolate is firm, sandwich the fingers with rose butter cream or flavoured whipped cream.

makes 8 to 12

50 g/2 oz/¼ cup caster sugar

1 tablespoon rose petal sugar – see p.20

2 large eggs, *beaten with* a tablespoon of rosewater *or* a couple of drops of rose culinary essence

75 g/3 oz/¾ cup self-raising flour

1 tablespoon dried rose petals (optional)

Orange blossom Jaffa cakes

I once lived near the highly fragrant McVitie factory where Jaffa cakes have been made since the late 1920s and would hear stories from schoolfriends who took holiday jobs there and were allowed to eat all the biscuits they wanted. Jaffa cakes, of course, are not biscuits, but cakes, as decided by a court ruling in 1991 when the company won a case against Her Majesty's Customs and Excise who wanted to charge Value Added Tax on them as biscuits. Surprisingly, the name is not a registered trademark.

My orange blossom version works very well, and is not difficult to make, even though the cake requires three stages, the sponge, the orange and the chocolate covering. I have made several versions of this recipe, including making my own orange jelly with gelatine, but a well-set good-quality orange marmalade without too much peel is as good as anything, and the slight bitterness of the marmalade is a nice foil to the sweet sponge and rich chocolate.

Grease eighteen 6 cm/2 ½ inch bun tins.

Whisk the sugar and egg until light and creamy. Add the butter and orange zest, then carefully fold in the flour.

Place soupspoons of the mixture in the greased bun tins, about half-filling them. Bake in a hot oven – 200°C/400°F/gas mark 6 – for about 5 to 8 minutes. Transfer to a wire rack to cool.

Meanwhile, melt the chocolate in a bowl set over hot water and put to one side to cool but not harden.

makes 18

75 g/3 oz/⅓ cup caster sugar

2 large eggs, *beaten with*

1 tablespoon orange flower water

1 tablespoon unsalted butter, melted

finely grated zest of 2 mandarins or 1 orange

75 g/3 oz/¾ cup self-raising flour

best quality orange marmalade

200 g/7 oz orange-flavoured dark chocolate

When the cakes are cool, return them to the bun tins. Spoon about a teaspoon of marmalade on each cake and put the tray in the refrigerator to chill the topping – this helps the chocolate set more quickly.

Remove the cakes from the refrigerator and spoon the chocolate over the top. It should begin to set almost immediately on contact with the chilled tin and the topping. Put in a cool place, but not in the fridge, for the chocolate to set completely before serving.

Cook's tip

If you cannot find orange-flavoured dark chocolate, stir finely grated mandarin or orange zest into the melted chocolate.

A lovely version of this cake can be made with roses and strawberries. Mix a tablespoon or so of freeze-dried strawberry pieces in the cake batter, along with a tablespoon of rosewater in place of orange flower water with the eggs. Spoon rose petal jelly on top of the cooled cakes and, once chilled, coat with melted white chocolate. The name Jaffa cake will have to go, however.

Cup cakes and fairy cakes

Named for the small paper cases in which they were traditionally baked, cup cakes have come back into fashion in recent years, appearing in every smart cake shop and department store bakery, in every farmers' market and on every Women's Institute stall. No Christmas Fair or summer fête was complete without a multi-hued array of these highly decorated small sponge cakes. And that supermarket bakery sections have greatly extended their range is in part due to all the many decorations they have devised for cup cakes, from shards of freeze-dried strawberries, fruit flake confetti, sparkling snow, 'shimmer sugar' and 'stardust' to ready-made icing flowers and butterflies. The same shelves also offer edible gold leaf, which used only to be available from specialist art suppliers – perfect for the Golden Celebration Cake on p.148.

Cup cakes are easy to make and very pretty and, above all, beautifully lend themselves to floral scented baking.

You can use the following recipe as a blueprint and branch out from there. You might flavour and colour the cake batter with rose petal or lavender sugar or a drop of floral essence, or you may simply want to use the colour and flavouring in the butter cream or frosting, using the recipe on p.23.

Basic cup cake recipe

Place 12 paper cases on a baking sheet or in a dozen 8 cm/3 inch bun tins.

You can use an electric hand-held mixer for this. Beat the eggs and sugar until light and fluffy. Gradually add the butter, beating continuously. Fold in the flour until you have a smooth batter. Distribute the mixture evenly into the prepared cases and bake at 180°C/350°F/gas mark 4 for 15 minutes. Leave for a few minutes and then transfer the cakes in their paper cases to cool on a wire rack. Decorate them only when completely cold.

makes 12 cup cakes

2 large eggs
115 g/4 oz/½ cup caster sugar
115 g/4 oz/1 stick unsalted butter, melted
115 g/4 oz/1 cup self-raising flour, sifted

Orange fairy cakes with fairy butter

Fairy cakes are a version of the cup cake and these used to be made for tea parties when I was a child. So-called because the top of the cake would be neatly hollowed out in a round, this would be cut in half, the hollow filled with butter cream and the two pieces of sponge neatly perched on top to represent wings.

Fairy cakes can be smaller and more delicate than cup cakes, so the same amount as the cup cake recipe will make about 18 fairy cakes. Rose, violet and lavender can be used to vary the recipe, with the appropriate flower water or culinary essence.

Place eighteen paper cases on a baking sheet or in eighteen 6 cm/2½ inch bun tins.

Beat the eggs and sugar until light and fluffy. Gradually add the butter, beating continuously. Stir in the orange zest. Fold in the flour until you have a smooth batter. Distribute the mixture evenly into the prepared cases and bake at 180°C/350°F/gas mark 4 for 15 minutes. Leave for a few minutes and then transfer the cakes in their paper cases to cool on a wire rack. When completely cold, carefully scoop out a round from the top of each cake as described above.

Gently, without squashing the tiny curls, spoon a little fairy butter into the hollow, perch the 'wings' on top and dust with a veil of icing sugar before serving.

makes 18

2 large eggs, *beaten with*
2 tablespoons orange flower water
115 g/4 oz/½ cup caster sugar
115 g/4 oz/1 stick unsalted butter, melted
grated zest of 1 mandarin or orange
115 g/4 oz/1 cup self-raising flour, sifted
fairy butter – see below
icing sugar

Fairy butter

This is based on a traditional eighteenth-century recipe and, as well as the perfect decoration for orange fairy cakes, I suggest this as an alternative to clotted cream when you are serving warm scones for tea. It is also good with griddle cakes, crumpets and all similarly nostalgic tea breads.

And of course, with a tint of pink food colouring and rosewater in place of orange flower water, you have rose fairy butter for rose petal fairy cakes.

Pound the egg yolks with the liquid and the icing sugar then thoroughly mix with the sugar. When well mixed, let the butter firm up slightly in the refrigerator and then push it through a sieve, letting it fall loosely in a heap.

**makes about 115 g/4 oz/
1 cup, loosely packed**

yolks only of 2 large hard-boiled eggs
1 tablespoon orange flower water
1 tablespoon icing sugar
50 g/2 oz/½ stick unsalted butter, at room temperature

Biscuits and shortbreads

There are occasions when one really does want just a cup of tea and a biscuit, rather than a full afternoon tea. Here are recipes for those occasions, especially the Garsington lavender shortbread and the lavender chocolate and almond biscuits.

One or two recipes that follow, such as the lavender and white chocolate caramel cake and the lemon and lavender squares, are rather more elaborate, but, being constructed on a shortbread base, this is where they belong.

Here is where you will find a recipe for Melting Moments, to be enhanced with the floral essence of your choice, and the delicate Lavender Kisses, based on an old family favourite.

Some of the biscuits, especially those based on the classic brandy snap recipe, are the perfect accompaniment to desserts such as fools and possets, ice-creams and sorbets.

"These are as attractive and as delicious as French macaroons, but far easier to make. In fact, in our house, the 'kiss' is the new macaroon."

Lavender kisses, p.92

Saffron, Cheddar and sesame biscuits

Home-made cheese biscuits could not be simpler, and your guests will be very impressed that you have baked them yourself. Using the same proportions, you can make up a much larger batch of mixture and freeze several cylinders of dough for use when needed.

Rub the butter and flour together, stir in the cheese, saffron and its water and seeds, adding a little water if necessary to bind the ingredients to a firm dough. Roll out the pastry and stamp out 5 cm/2 inch discs. Place on baking sheets and bake at 180°C/350°F/gas mark 4 for 8 to 10 minutes. Cool on wire racks before storing in an airtight container.

Cook's tip

To prepare in advance, roll the raw mixture into a cylinder, wrap well and freeze. Cut off thin slices to bake as and when you need them.

makes 24

115 g/4 oz/1 stick butter
115 g/4 oz/1 cup plain flour
115 g/4 oz/1 cup Cheddar, grated
$\frac{1}{20}$ g/25 saffron threads soaked in 1 tablespoon boiling water
1 tablespoon sesame seeds

Wild garlic flower, walnut and Lancashire cheese biscuits

Another version of cheese biscuits, these are a springtime recipe, when wild garlic can be foraged on heaths and in hedgerows. Use the tender leaves raw in salads, the tougher leaves in soup and pesto and the flowers in all manner of baked goods – see pp.118 and 123 for more ideas. Strip the individual star-like flowers from the flower head and then chop the stems as you would with chives.

Rub the butter and flour together, stir in the cheese, walnuts and wild garlic flowers and chopped stems, adding a little water to bind the ingredients to a firm dough. Roll out the pastry and stamp out 5 cm/2 inch discs. Preheat your oven to 180°C/350°F/gas mark 4. Place on baking sheets and bake for 8 to 10 minutes. Cool on wire racks before storing in an airtight container. Alternatively, trim the pastry into a neat rectangle, cut into strips and twist. Or cut into wider strips and then into diamonds or triangles.

Cook's tip

To prepare in advance, roll the raw mixture into a cylinder, wrap well and freeze and cut off thin slices to bake as you need them.

makes about 24

115 g/4 oz/1 stick butter

115 g/4 oz/1 cup plain flour

115 g/4 oz/1 cup Lancashire cheese, crumbled

2 tablespoons walnuts, well-crushed but not pulverised

12 stems wild garlic flowers – see recipe

1 to 2 tablespoons cold water – see recipe

Fennel flower and Parmesan twists

You can adapt the recipe to saffron; in which case, beat the egg with 1 tablespoon water in which you have infused $1/20$ g/25 threads of saffron.

Mix flour and salt and rub in the fat. Stir in the grated cheese and make into a stiff paste with the milk and egg mixture. Roll out very thinly and cut into narrow fingers. Prick with a fork, carefully twist them and place on a lined baking sheet. Bake at 180–190°C/350–375°F/gas mark 4–5 for 15 to 20 minutes until well browned.

makes about 3 dozen

225 g/8 oz/2 cups self-raising flour

a pinch of salt

75 g/3 oz/¾ stick butter

115 g/4 oz/1 cup Parmesan, grated

1 egg, *beaten with*

1 tablespoon milk

1 teaspoon fennel flowers

Lavender, sun-dried tomato and olive biscuits

These savoury biscuits are full of the flavours of Provence, delicious with an aperitif.

Using the same proportions, you can make up a much larger batch of mixture and freeze several cylinders of dough for use when needed.

Rub the butter and flour together, stir in the cheese, tomato, olives and lavender, adding a little water to bind the ingredients to a firm dough. Preheat your oven to 180°C/350°F/ gas mark 4. Roll out the pastry and stamp out 5 cm/2 inch discs. Place on baking sheets and bake for 8 to 10 minutes. Cool on wire racks before storing in an airtight container.

makes 24

115 g / 4 oz / 1 stick butter
115 g / 4 oz / 1 cup plain flour
115 g / 4 oz / 1 cup Parmesan, grated
4 pieces sun-dried tomato, finely chopped
6 black olives, stoned, well-drained and finely chopped
1 teaspoon lavender flowers
water – see recipe

Cook's tip

To prepare in advance, roll the raw mixture into a cylinder, wrap well and freeze and cut off thin slices to bake as you need them.

Saffron and rosewater biscuits

Saffron and rosewater is a subtle and pleasing combination, found in much traditional baking, especially from Devon and Cornwall.

Line 2 or 3 baking sheets with silicone or baking parchment.

Cream the butter and sugar until pale and fluffy. Beat in the egg and then add the milk, saffron and its liquid, rosewater and cardamom. Mix in the dry ingredients until you have a stiff dough. Roll out on a floured surface, and cut into 4 cm/1 ½ inch rounds.

makes about 3 dozen

225 g / 8 oz / 2 sticks unsalted butter at room temperature
225 g / 8 oz / 1 cup caster sugar
1 egg, *beaten with*
2–3 teaspoons rosewater
75 ml / 3 fl oz / ⅓ cup milk
¹⁄₂₀ g / 25 threads saffron infused in 1 tablespoon boiling water
a pinch of ground cardamom

Place on baking sheets and chill for 15 to 20 minutes in the refrigerator before baking in a preheated oven at 160°C/325°F/gas mark 3 for about 30 minutes. Cool on a wire rack.

150 g/5 oz/1 ¼ cups plain flour
25 g/1 oz/⅙ cup ground rice
50 g/2 oz/⅓ cup ground almonds

Lavender snaps

This and the next recipe are based on the classic brandy snap, made crisp with the addition of Golden Syrup. Once the biscuits are baked, you need to work fairly quickly to ensure that the snaps are cool enough to handle yet not too firm to mould round the wooden handle. You can also mould them on a greased rolling pin, which will give you a more open shell, a *tuile*, that you can fill with fruit and cream, or simply serve with coffee or at teatime.

Heat the butter, sugar and Golden Syrup in a small heavy saucepan until the butter has melted. Remove from the heat and mix in the rest of the ingredients. Drop very small spoonfuls of the mixture on the sheet, well spaced as they will spread. Bake in a preheated oven at 180°C/350°F/gas mark 4 for 8 to 10 minutes until golden brown and lacy.

Remove from the oven and, when firm enough, after a minute or two, lift off the baking sheet and shape while still warm and pliable round the greased wooden handle. When set, gently remove and cool on wire racks. I like them quite plain like this, but you can pipe lavender-scented whipped cream or butter cream into the snaps, or serve them with clotted cream.

makes 20

50 g/2 oz/½ stick unsalted butter
50 g/2 oz/¼ cup caster sugar or light muscovado sugar
5 teaspoons Golden Syrup
50 g/2 oz/½ cup plain flour, sifted
¼ teaspoon lavender flowers
zest of half a lemon, grated
a drop of culinary lavender essence – optional

Orange flower and almond crisps

With orange flower water and almonds, there is a hint of the Mediterranean in this and the next, very different, recipe.

Line or grease two baking sheets.

Sift the dry ingredients together, stir in the sugar and rub in the butter. Mix to a paste with the syrup, orange zest and juice, and orange flower water. Roll into large walnut-sized balls and place on the baking sheets, well spaced. Flatten slightly and scatter the almonds on top. Bake at 180°C/350°F/gas mark 4 for 15 to 20 minutes until light golden brown. Cool on wire racks.

makes about 36

225 g/8 oz/2 cups self-
 raising flour
¼ teaspoon ground
 cardamom
½ tsp bicarbonate of soda
115 g/4 oz/½ cup light
 muscovado sugar
115 g/4 oz/1 stick unsalted
 butter
4 tablespoons Golden Syrup
zest of 1 orange and
 1 tablespoon of juice
1 tablespoon orange flower
 water
75 g/3 oz/½ cup flaked
 almonds

Orange snaps

Line 2 or 3 baking sheets with silicone or baking parchment and grease the narrow handles of wooden spoons to shape the biscuits.

Heat the butter, sugar and Golden Syrup in a small heavy saucepan until the butter has melted. Remove from the heat and mix in the rest of the ingredients. Line a baking sheet with silicone paper and drop very small spoonfuls of the mixture on the sheet, well spaced. Bake in a preheated oven at 180°C/350°F/gas mark 4 for 8 to 10 minutes until golden brown and lacy.

Remove from the oven and, when firm enough, after a minute or two, lift off the

makes 20

50 g/2 oz/½ stick unsalted
 butter
50 g/2 oz/¼ cup caster or
 light muscovado sugar
5 teaspoons Golden Syrup
50 g/2 oz/½ cup plain flour,
 sifted
1 tablespoon orange flower
 water
2 teaspoons grated orange,
 mandarin or tangerine rind

baking sheet and shape while still warm and pliable round the greased wooden handle. When set, gently remove and cool on wire racks. Fill with a rosette of orange flower-scented butter cream in each end.

Orange flower crescents

These pale, delicate and scented shortbread-like biscuits will accompany a tangerine sorbet or ice-cream to perfection. It is important not to let them brown.

Line or grease two baking sheets.

Rub the flour and butter together, add the sugar, almonds, zest and orange flower water, kneading to a stiff paste. Roll out to about 1 cm/½ inch thick and carefully transfer to baking sheets. Bake for 30 minutes at 150°C/300°F/gas mark 2. Transfer to wire racks to cool and sprinkle with caster sugar while hot.

The same method can be used for other floral scented crescents.

makes about 18

200 g/7 oz/1 ¾ cups plain flour
175 g/6 oz/1 ½ sticks unsalted butter
50 g/2 oz/¼ cup caster, plus extra – see recipe
75 g/3 oz/½ cup ground almonds
zest of 1 orange
1 tablespoon orange flower water

Lavender, chocolate and almond biscuits

Line two baking sheets with silicone or baking parchment.

Cream the butter and sugar, then beat in the egg and fold in the flour. Stir the chocolate and almonds into the mixture, as well as the lavender essence, if using it.

Scoop up walnut-sized balls with floured hands and place them on two prepared baking sheets,

makes 2 dozen

150 g/5 oz/1 ¼ sticks unsalted butter
100 g/4 oz/½ cup caster sugar
50 g/2 oz/¼ cup lavender sugar – see p.20
1 egg

well spaced. Press down with fingers, or spatula, to a diameter of about 7.5 cm/3 inches, and bake for 12 to 15 minutes in a preheated oven at 180°C/350°F/gas mark 4. Remove from the oven, leave for a minute or two and then cool the biscuits on a wire rack to crisp them up.

Alternatively, roll the mixture into a cylinder, wrap well and freeze until required. Thaw out slightly and slice the dough, arranging the rounds on baking sheets and baking as above.

200 g/7 oz/1¾ cups plain flour
75 g/3 oz good quality dark chocolate plus a drop of culinary lavender essence
or
75 g/3 oz/¾ cup lavender chocolate, chopped or coarsely grated
¾ cup/75 g/3 oz flaked almonds

Rich lemon and lavender biscuits

Line or grease a baking sheet.

Mix the flour and sugar, rub in the butter. Beat in the juice, zest and egg. Roll out thinly on a floured worktop and cut with fluted pastry cutter. Place on the baking sheet and bake at 180°C/350°F/gas mark 4 for about 15 minutes. Cool on a wire rack.

makes 24 to 30

225 g/8 oz/2 cups self-raising flour
50 g/2 oz/¼ cup caster sugar
50 g/2 oz/¼ cup lavender sugar – see p.20
115 g/4 oz butter/1 stick unsalted butter
1 egg beaten with the rind of 1 lemon and half its juice

Lavender and white chocolate caramel cake

This is based on my mother's recipe for toffee cake, given to her by a neighbour when my brother and I were teenagers, so it has been around since at least the early 1960s, although online references claim that the earliest sightings of this rich indulgence were in the 1970s and 80s. The cake is now better than ever because we can get such good chocolate. It is not difficult to appreciate how the newer name of Millionaire's shortbread came about; that version has a dark chocolate topping swirled with milk chocolate and white chocolate.

Lightly butter a 20 cm/8 inch cake tin, about 4 cm/1½ inches deep, or a tin of roughly the same size.

Press the shortbread dough into the tin and bake in a preheated oven at 190–200°C/ 375–400°F/gas mark 5–6 for 12 to 15 minutes. Remove the tin from the oven and leave the shortbread in it.

To make the toffee, pour the Golden Syrup and condensed milk into a saucepan, stir together over moderate heat until well-mixed, then boil for precisely 7 minutes, stirring all the time.

Spread the mixture over the shortbread and allow it to cool. Melt the chocolate in a bowl over hot water, mix in the essence and spread over the cooled toffee, marking into small triangles, squares or fingers, as appropriate, before the chocolate has set. Cut when cold.

makes 16

Shortbread
115 g/4 oz/½ cup plain flour
25 g/1 oz/1 tablespoon
    lavender sugar – see p.20
50 g/2 oz/½ stick unsalted
    butter, melted

Topping
2 tablespoons Golden Syrup
395 g/14 oz can condensed
    milk
200 g/7 oz high-quality white
    chocolate
a drop of culinary lavender
    essence – see p.14

Lemon and lavender squares

Based on another family recipe, this time from America, this is a very good teatime pastry; it is like eating shortbread topped with lemon curd. The squares are made in two stages, first the shortbread and then the lemon topping.

Lightly butter a 20 cm/8 inch square cake tin.

Sift the first quantity of flour and icing sugar together and mix in the melted butter with a

makes 16
115 g/4 oz/½ cup plain flour
25 g/1 oz/2 tablespoons
    icing sugar, plus extra for
    sifting – see recipe
50 g/2 oz/½ stick unsalted
    butter, melted
2 tablespoons plain flour

fork. Press into the cake tin and bake for 20 minutes in a preheated oven at 180°C/350°F/ gas mark 4.

Beat the remaining ingredients together until smooth and lump free, then pour over the hot crust. Return to the oven for 25 minutes. Remove from the oven and, when cool, sift generously with icing sugar, cut into squares and serve.

2 large eggs

4 tablespoons lemon juice

2 teaspoons grated lemon zest

4 tablespoons lavender sugar – see p.20

½ teaspoon baking powder

Garsington lavender shortbread

The terrace of Garsington Manor used to be lined with a dense border of lavender when I spent some time there as a consultant for the opera season menus, so inspiration for this shortbread recipe was not hard to find. We served it with gooseberry fool originally, and I recommend it with any fruit fool, ice-cream or sorbet, especially lavender of course.

Cream the butter and sugar, stir in the flour, and add just enough water to make a stiff pastry. Roll out on a floured worktop to about 1 cm/½ inch thick. Cut into fingers or rounds. Bake for 20 to 30 minutes at 170°C/325°F/ gas mark 3 and – 5 minutes before removing from the oven – dust with caster sugar. Cool on a wire rack.

makes about 30

115 g/4 oz/1 stick unsalted butter

75 g/3 oz/ ⅓ cup lavender sugar – see p.20

150 g/6 oz/1 ⅔ cup plain flour, sifted

iced water, if required

caster sugar for dusting

Rose-scented petticoat tails

These are miniature versions of Scottish short-bread petticoat tails, so-called because of their shape.

Cream the butter and sugar, stir in the

makes 3 to 4 dozen

115 g/4 oz/1 stick unsalted butter

50 g/2 oz/scant ½ cup icing sugar, sifted

flour and ground rice, and add just enough rosewater to make a stiff paste. Roll out to ½ cm/¼ inch thick. Cut into 7.5 cm/3 inch circles, and then cut a 1 cm/½ inch round from the centre of each. Mark each circle into 6 to 8 wedges with a knife cut, and prick a design with a fork or skewer. Bake for 20 to 30 minutes at 170°C/325°F/gas mark 3. Five minutes before removing from the oven, dust with the extra rose petal sugar. Cool the biscuits on a wire rack.

25 g/1 oz/1 tablespoon rose petal sugar, plus extra for sifting – see recipe; see p.20
150 g/5 oz/1¼ cups plain flour, sifted
25 g/1 oz/1 tablespoon ground rice
rosewater – see recipe

Lavender crunchies

The crunch in these easy teatime bakemeats comes from the Golden Syrup and the oatmeal.

Line with baking parchment or grease a baking sheet.

Cream the fats and sugar. Add syrup, boiling water and a drop of lavender essence. Stir in the flour and the oats. Roll into generous walnut-sized balls. Place on the prepared baking sheet and bake at 160–180°C/325–350°F/gas mark 3–4 for 15 to 20 minutes. When cold, these can be iced with a lavender water ice, made by mixing sifted icing sugar with a little lemon juice and a drop of culinary lavender essence.

makes 12

50 g/2 oz/4 tablespoons lard
50 g/2 oz/½ stick butter
3 oz/75 g/⅓ cup caster sugar
1 teaspoon Golden Syrup
1 tablespoon boiling water
culinary lavender essence – see p.14
115 g/4 oz/1 cup self-raising flour
50 g/2 oz/⅔ cup rolled oats

Melting moments

The 'austerity' 1950s version of the recipe on which this is based calls for the pastries to be rolled in oatmeal or desiccated coconut. They are even better with almonds. The way I like to prepare the nuts for this is to take flaked almonds and process them briefly so that I am left with small flakes; I prefer this texture to that of chopped whole almonds.

Line with baking parchment or grease a baking sheet.

Cream the fat and sugar, beat in the egg and lavender essence, stir in the flour and mix thoroughly. Wet your hands and form mixture into balls the size of large marbles. Roll in oats or coconut. Place on the baking sheet and press out slightly. Bake at 150–180°C/325–350°F/ gas mark 3–4 for 15 to 20 minutes. A glacé cherry was always the traditional decoration, but I use a crystallised lavender bud instead, placed on as soon as the biscuits come out of the oven and before they have set.

makes 18

75 g/3 oz/⅓ cup caster sugar
75 g/3 oz/¾ unsalted butter
25 g/1 oz/2 tablespoons lard
1 small egg
culinary lavender essence – see p.14
150 g/5 oz/1¼ cups self-raising flour
flaked almonds – see recipe

Lavender kisses

One probably should not have favourite recipes, but if I did, this one would come close. It is based on the little cakes my mother used to make for special occasions, such as a visit from her mother-in-law and her mother in law's own mother. The original recipe, from her much battered and spattered 1950s Be-Ro recipe booklet, was for coffee kisses. It translates beautifully into tender floral mouthfuls, sealed with a kiss of floral butter cream; for the recipe works equally well with roses and violets.

These are as attractive and as delicious as French macaroons, but *far* easier to make. In fact, in our house, the kiss is the new macaroon.

makes about 20

175 g/6 oz/1½ cups self-raising flour
50 g/2 oz/¼ cup caster sugar
25 g/1 oz/1 tablespoon lavender sugar – see p.20
75 g/3 oz/¾ stick unsalted butter
1 egg, *beaten with*
2 or 3 drops culinary lavender essence – see p.14

Mix the flour and sugar, then rub in the butter. Stir in the egg and lavender essence. This makes quite a soft mixture, especially if working in a warm kitchen, so you might want to chill it for half an hour or so in the fridge. Form into marble-sized balls. Place on a well-greased baking sheet. Bake at 160–180°C/325–350°F/gas mark 3–4 for 15 to 20 minutes. Cool on a wire rack and, when cold, sandwich with the lavender butter cream made by mixing the filling ingredients together.

Filling
50 g/2 oz/scant ½ cup icing
    sugar
culinary lavender essence –
    see p.14
25 g/1 oz/¼ stick butter,
    softened
a dash of purple food
    colouring

Floral-scented Catherine wheels

Line or grease a baking sheet

makes 12 to 15

Cream the sugar and butter until pale and creamy, add the flour and egg and whichever floral essence you choose. Divide the mixture in two. With one piece knead in the cocoa thoroughly and roll out to a rectangle about 1 cm/½ inch thick. Sprinkle with caster sugar. Roll out the second piece to the same size and place it on top of the first one. Lightly pass a rolling pin over the top and trim the edges. Sprinkle with more caster sugar. Roll up tightly, loosely cover and keep in a cool place for half an hour. Cut into ½ cm/¼ inch slices with a sharp knife, place on the baking sheet and bake for about 15 to 20 minutes at 190°C/375°F/gas mark 5. Cool on a wire rack.

115 g/4 oz/½ cup caster
    sugar – plus extra, see
    recipe
115 g/4 oz/1 stick butter
225 g/8 oz/2 cups self-
    raising flour
1 small egg, lightly beaten
floral essence – see recipe
1 tablespoon cocoa

Rose fingerprint biscuits

For an easy-to-make biscuit, these are hard to top. Add some ground almonds and fill them with apricot jam for an elegant teatime treat; use lemon zest and lemon curd for biscuits to serve with ice-cream. Or simply fill with strawberry jam for a bedtime treat with a glass of milk. They are equally at home in lunch boxes.

Grease or line two baking sheets with baking parchment.

Beat the butter and sugar until pale and fluffy, add any zest or flavouring at this stage, then fold in the flour with a metal spoon until the mixture combines to a soft dough. Take a small piece of dough and roll it into a generous walnut-sized ball. Place on the baking tray and continue with the rest of the dough, leaving space between each as the mixture spreads during baking.

Using your finger, make an imprint in each ball, big enough to hold about a teaspoon of rose petal jelly.

Bake in a preheated oven at 180°C/350°F/ gas mark 4 for 15 to 20 minutes until light golden brown. Carefully transfer the biscuits to a wire rack to cool completely.

makes 2 to 3 dozen

225 g/8 oz/2 sticks unsalted butter, softened

50 g/2 oz/¼ cup caster sugar

50 g/2 oz/¼ cup rose petal sugar – see p.20

300 g/10 oz/1 ½ cups plain flour, *sifted with*

½ tsp baking powder

8 tbsp rose petal jelly – see p.22

Meringues, *macarons* and éclairs

One visit I made to Paris some years ago required me to take an apple corer. My task, the next morning starting at 6.30, was to core and bake 150 Cox's apples for a gala dinner that night, a celebration of British food cooked by the British for the French. Over the previous few months, I had spent a good deal of time with Claire Clark, one of the world's top pastry chefs, in her kitchen. The two of us had been paired to take responsibility for bread, pudding and sweetmeats. As this was to be a British meal, any notion of *petits fours* was banished. What we came up with was a selection of dainty, miniaturised versions of treacle tarts and shortbread, real fruit jellies and macaroons. We know they were appealing because at our various test meals there were never any left over.

It was a privilege and a delight to work in Claire's kitchen, with its calm, cool atmosphere and Claire's firm, straightforward guidance of her team, her lively curiosity and her high standards. From then on, whenever I made sweetmeats and other delicate confections,

"A lavender water ice with a chocolate lavender custard filling is very good, as is the reverse, a chocolate topping with a lavender custard filling."

Rose petal éclairs, p.115

I did not tag them onto a longer cooking session, but made them the focus. That way, I had a better chance of a cool, dry kitchen, cool equipment and a cool worktop. I could work without hurrying, develop a rhythm, concentrate and discipline myself to weigh and measure accurately.

The recipes in this chapter are amongst the most delicate in the book, especially the meringues and the French almond macaroons, and they benefit from this discipline I learned in Claire's kitchen.

And on a further practical note, a good supply of rice paper or silicone, or heavy-duty non-stick bakeware is useful. Sugar and flour should be sifted. And it is vital that if you are using nuts, ground or otherwise, they should be absolutely fresh. Rancid nuts impart a disagreeable flavour. If you need to grease trays or tins, then a neutral oil like groundnut is best; butter or almond oil can also be used.

Three basic recipes

Choux paste

Choux pastry or *pâte à choux* is a very useful recipe to have in the repertoire, for it can play a part in a variety of dishes, from *amuse-bouches* to *petits fours*, from *pâtisserie* to *pièces montées*. Chocolate éclairs, cream buns, profiteroles, *gâteau St Honoré*, *religieuses*, Paris-Brests, *croquembouche* and *salambo* as well as savoury choux buns and *gougère*, all require a choux paste to begin with. For this is properly a paste and not a pastry.

**makes 1 large choux ring,
8 individual choux buns or
24 small ones**

115 ml/4 oz/½ cup water
2 oz/50 g/½ stick butter
a pinch of salt
75 g/3 oz/¾ cup plain flour
2 eggs, lightly beaten

If you do not have the cool hands and marble worktop of the professional pastry cook, do not worry. With choux paste, the ingredients are boiled in a saucepan, and this produces feather-light results.

Lightly grease a baking sheet.

Bring the water, butter and salt to the boil in a small, heavy-based saucepan and, when it does so, tip in all the flour at once, stirring vigorously with a wooden spoon. As you stir, the mixture will dry and become smooth to the point where it leaves the sides of the pan. Remove from the heat and beat in the eggs, a little at a time, making sure each addition is thoroughly incorpo-rated. Because the absorbent quality of flour can change from batch to batch and can vary with the day's humidity, it is a good idea not to add the whole of the second egg, as you may not need it all to give you a soft, pliable but not liquid dough. On the other hand, if the flour is very dry, you may need to add a little more beaten egg. At this point, too, add any flavourings. Keep stirring until you have a smooth paste.

The mixture can be kept now for use later. If you wish to do this, cover the surface with damp greaseproof paper to stop a crust forming. Otherwise, proceed immediately.

The oven should be heated to 180°C/350°F/gas mark 4. Spoon or pipe the paste in small heaps, larger heaps or sausage shapes, depending on what you wish to make, onto the baking sheet with space between, as they expand on baking. Bake for about 10 to 15 minutes for small buns, 25 to 30 minutes for a *gougère* or a Paris-Brest. Turn off the heat and allow to cool with the door of the oven open. Remove from the oven, split and fill with your chosen filling.

Floral meringues

To ensure maximum volume for the egg white, it is essential to have a scrupulously clean bowl and no specks of egg yolk in the white. Even the slightest film of grease will prevent it attaining its full volume. Meringues are notoriously tricky to make if you are working in a humid atmosphere, because one is drying them as much as baking them.

Line a baking sheet with non-stick baking parchment or a special baking mat.

Put the egg white in a large bowl. Sprinkle on a tablespoon of sugar and begin whisking. When the egg white is foamy and increased in volume, add half the remaining sugar and continue whisking. At this point add any culinary floral essence and colouring. The meringue will begin to take shape, becoming glossy and with smaller bubbles. Continue whisking until you have added all the sugar and the meringue is now a firm mass of glossy foam, with tiny bubbles. When you trail the whisk through it, the mixture will peak and hold its shape.

Spoon or pipe the meringue into four nests or baskets on the prepared baking sheet, with a depression in the middle. Bake – or rather, dry – in a preheated oven at 125°C/250°F/ gas mark ½ for about 45 minutes. Turn off the heat and leave the oven door ajar until the meringues are completely dry. Remove the now cold meringues from the oven and store in an airtight tin until required.

makes 4

1 large egg white
115 g/4 oz/½ cup caster
    sugar
culinary floral essence such
    as rose or lavender –
    see p.14
food colouring – as
    appropriate

Variations

Quantities can be increased by simple multiplication.
For filled meringues, pipe or spoon into heaps on the
baking sheet and, when cooked and cooled, sandwich with
whipped cream. Ivory-coloured meringues can be achieved
by using light muscovado sugar. A little cocoa powder
can be whisked in with the final addition of sugar to make
chocolate meringues. Fill them with floral scented whipped
cream, butter cream or pastry cream – see p.94.

Macarons – almond macaroons

The French *macaron* is a very delicate confection of ground almonds, sugar and egg white,
which was made fashionable some years ago by
Pierre Hermé, when he developed countless
flavours and colours for the pastry while
working at Ladurée, the famous Paris *pâtisserie*.
But the *macaron* is a traditional French pastry.
The original *macaron de Saint Emilion* was made
in the Ursulines convent in Saint Emilion in
1620, to the same basic recipe of egg white,
ground almonds and sugar. When at the Revo-
lution the nuns had to leave the convent, they
passed the recipe to a local family, so history
has it, and the *macarons* are still made today
in the village, a more rustic, golden-baked
version of the stylish pastry you will now find
in *pâtisseries* all over the world, and which
originated in Hermé's home town of Nancy.

There are several essential points to achieving
success. The egg whites are best when not too
fresh and can be near their 'use by' date when
they are more liquid. The whisked mixture
must be glossy and smooth, with no air
bubbles from egg white whisked too loosely.
The *macarons* should be left to dry before

makes about 20

150 g/5 oz/1 cup finely
    ground almonds
225 g/8 oz/1⅔ cups icing
    sugar, plus 1 tbsp
115 ml/4 oz/just over ½ cup
    egg whites (from 4 or 5
    eggs)
1 teaspoon dried egg white
    powder – optional but
    useful for the texture

baking, which will ensure a crisp shell and the characteristic 'foot' or 'frill' at the base.
A piping bag with a round nozzle will help you achieve perfection.

Line baking sheets with silicone for ease of removal.

Sift the ground almonds and measured sugar together. Whisk the egg whites and, as they firm up, sprinkle in the powdered egg white and the extra tablespoon of sugar, whisking until the mixture is firm and glossy. Add a tablespoon or so of the almond and sugar mixture to the egg white and fold in gently, and then gently fold in the remaining dry ingredients, which should finish with the consistency of a soft, glossy paste.

Pipe into small rounds, about 2.5 cm/1 inch apart, on the baking sheets and bang the tray to get rid of any air bubbles. This is best done by putting a tea towel on the work top and dropping the baking tray straight down. Let the *macarons* dry for about an hour in a dry place before baking at 180°C/350°F/gas mark 4 for 8 minutes. Turn the tray around and bake for another 7 minutes. Allow to cool, then sandwich with the butter cream or the filling of your choice.

Milk chocolate lavender teacakes

Baking and nostalgia, the two seem to go together. I often find myself making the cakes and biscuits I remember from childhood, or the pastries and pies I have baked with friends and family in their kitchens over the years. I saw a mould for chocolate teacakes in the Lakeland catalogue, together with a recipe, and realised I was not the only one experiencing nostalgia for baked treats past, and had to try my hand at them. The lavender is my own addition, and you can readily adapt the recipe to make rose chocolate teacakes.

To make them you need a silicone mould with six 7.5 cm/3 inch half spheres. And a hand-held beater or mixer will make light work of the marshmallow filling, at least. Chocolate teacakes are not something to be undertaken in a hurry, requiring several stages in the preparation, lining moulds with chocolate at just the right temperature, making shortbread-style biscuits to *exactly* fit the moulds, making a marshmallow filling of just the right consistency, assembling the teacakes, letting them set and then the delicate task of removing them from the mould.

Unlike most other recipes which suggest chocolate 'with cocoa solids of at least 70%', one with a lower percentage will work better here as the slightly softer texture will make removal from the mould easier. I recommend one of the premium milk chocolate bars, with 35 to 49% cocoa solids. The original chocolate teacakes were certainly made with milk chocolate.

makes 6

Chocolate

400 g/14 oz intense milk
    chocolate – see recipe

Biscuit

115 g/4 oz/1 cup plain flour,
    sifted with
a pinch of salt *and*
½ teaspoon baking powder
25 g/1 oz/1 tablespoon
    lavender sugar
25 g/1 oz/¼ stick unsalted
    butter
1 tablespoon beaten egg

Marshmallow

3 egg whites
150 g/5 oz/1 scant cup icing
    sugar
3 tablespoons liquid glucose,
    light corn syrup or Golden
    Syrup
½ teaspoon salt
a few drops of culinary
    lavender essence
2 or 3 drops of purple food
    colouring – optional

Preheat the oven to 160°C/325°F/gas mark 3. Silicone moulds are essential here, in order to remove the teacakes unblemished. Line or grease and flour a small baking sheet for the biscuits.

Melt 350 g/12 oz of the chocolate in a bowl set over hot water. Leave aside until it is no longer runny but will stick to the inside of the moulds.

To make the biscuits, put the dry ingredients in a bowl and rub in the butter until crumbly. Add the egg and mix together to form a smooth ball. Roll out the dough to about ½ cm/¼ inch thick on a floured worktop. Cut out six rounds with a 7.5 cm/3 inch plain, not fluted, cutter.

Place the rounds on the prepared baking sheet and refrigerate for 10 to 20 minutes. Bake the biscuits for about 12 minutes, remove from the oven and carefully transfer to a wire rack to cool and crisp up.

Coat the inside of the moulds with the melted chocolate using a firm brush, with the back of a spoon or, if you can wear thin latex gloves, with your fingers. It is important to get an even coating, so that the sides are firm enough to contain the mixture, but not too thick to make the teacakes difficult to eat. Leave the lined moulds to set in a cool place, but not the refrigerator, as this will spoil the appearance of the chocolate. Cover the cooled biscuits in the remaining melted chocolate and place on a silicone sheet or baking parchment.

For the marshmallow, place all of the ingredients in a large bowl set over a pan of simmering water, making sure the bottom of the bowl does not touch the water, as this would cook the egg whites. Here is where the electric whisk will be useful. The mixture needs to be whisked until doubled in volume, until there are stiff peaks, firm enough for piping, and the mass is smooth and glossy; 15 minutes or so by hand, half that with an electric whisk. Once it has reached the required volume and texture, scoop the marshmallow mixture into a piping bag.

To assemble the teacakes, melt the remainder of the chocolate and put to one side to firm up a little. Peel the biscuits off the parchment and place them onto clean parchment, chocolate side down. Pipe the marshmallow into each chocolate-lined mould just up to the top. Spread a little of the melted chocolate over the marshmallow and around the edge of each biscuit, which will serve to seal the two parts together as you quickly place a biscuit, chocolate-covered side uppermost, on top of the marshmallow. Smooth the still soft chocolate around the edges with a palette knife to cover the join. Leave the teacakes to set until completely cool and sealed together. Carefully remove the teacakes from the mould, place on a serving plate and keep in a cool place until required. My hat goes off to Mr Tunnock for such an extraordinary invention, and I hope he would not object to my floral addition.

Chocolate and lavender madeleines

Freshly baked madeleines are often served as *petits fours* at the end of dinner in restaurants. Because they bake so quickly, this is just about achievable at home, but also consider serving them as part of a 'chocolate tea' or *merienda*, that rather agreeable Spanish and South American tradition whereby hot chocolate is served in the late afternoon with a few pastries.

Preheat the oven to 220°C/450°F/gas mark 8. Butter and flour one or two trays of madeleine moulds.

Sift together the dry ingredients. Beat in the eggs and then mix in the melted butter. Pour the batter – and the mixture really is quite liquid – into the prepared moulds and bake in the top half of the oven for 5 to 7 minutes.

Remove from the oven once the madeleines are well-risen, and with the characteristic 'bump' in the middle. Serve while still warm, dusted with icing sugar or dipped into melted dark chocolate.

makes 24

50 g/2 oz/¼ cup lavender sugar – see p.20

50 g/2 oz/¼ cup caster sugar

75 g/3 oz/¾ cup self-raising flour

4 level teaspoons cocoa powder

half a coffeespoon of salt

2 eggs, lightly beaten

150 g/5 oz/1 ¼ sticks unsalted butter, melted

Linden flower and honey madeleines

For a true Proustian delight, serve these with a delicate china cup of *tilleul*, an infusion of linden flowers. Dried or fresh can be used. They are also excellent served with ice-cream made with the same linden flower honey.

Grease 48 madeleine moulds (or bake in several batches).

Bring the honey to the boil and stir in the linden flowers. Simmer for a few minutes and then remove from the heat and infuse for 15 minutes.

Strain the honey into a jug, or glass pot. You only need 2 soupspoons for the madeleines, but save the rest for spooning onto teatime scones or breakfast muffins.

Melt the butter in a saucepan and let it cool down. Beat the eggs, honey and sugar in a large bowl, or electric mixer, until very pale and thick.

Fold the sifted flour into the mixture, also gently pouring in most, about 200 g/7 oz, of the melted butter. Use the rest for greasing the madeleine moulds. Lightly dust with flour. Fill two-thirds full with the mixture and bake in a preheated oven at 220°C/450°F/gas mark 8 for about 5 to 8 minutes, until risen and golden brown. Turn out immediately to cool and serve while still warm.

makes 48

200 or 400 g/7 or 14 oz jar clear honey

25–50 g dried linden flowers (*tilleul*)

225 g/8 oz/2 sticks unsalted butter

5 eggs

75 g/3 oz/⅓ cup caster sugar

200 g/7 oz/1¾ cups self-raising flour, sifted

Orange, chocolate and coconut macaroons

These are very traditional teatime treats, which are completely unlike the French *macarons* (see p.99). Very simple to make, the dark chocolate and the orange flower water turn these into a rather sophisticated little treat.

Mix the coconut and sugar, add the orange flower water and enough egg white to bind together in a firm paste. Use a pair of dessert-spoons, dipped in water, to shape neat oval lozenges. Place them on a baking sheet, lined with rice paper and bake in a preheated oven at 160°C/325°F/gas mark 3 for about 15 to 20 minutes, until just pale gold. Remove from the

makes about 20

115 g/4 oz/1 cup desiccated coconut

115 g/4 oz/¾ cup icing sugar

2 to 3 teaspoons orange flower water

finely grated zest of 1 orange

1 egg white

crystallised orange peel for decoration, cut into very thin slivers

50 g/2 oz bar dark chocolate – at least 70% cocoa solids

oven, top each with two or three slivers orange peel and cool on a wire rack.

When the macaroons are cold, melt the chocolate, dip the base of each macaroon in the melted chocolate, and a little way up the side so that it will be visible. Place the macaroons on a wire rack, base uppermost, until the chocolate has set.

Hazelnut and lavender macaroons

I devised this recipe one Christmas when I was tired of looking at a depleted bowl of nuts and bored of cracking them, with bits of shell all over the table. So I cracked the whole lot and pulverised them in the food-processor, using them to make macaroons. The mixed nuts were fine, but even better was a second version made only with hazelnuts. Of course, one can now buy ground hazelnuts very readily, so these are a very easy option for afternoon tea.

Line a baking sheet with rice paper, greaseproof or silicone. Preheat the oven to 180°C/350°F, gas mark 4.

Mix the ground nuts and sugar together, then stir in the egg white to form a stiff paste. Roll marble-sized balls of the paste and arrange them on the prepared baking sheet, leaving about 2.5 cm/1 inch between the balls, which you then flatten gently with oiled fingers. The final size should be about 4 cm/1½ inches in diameter and about ½ cm/¼ inch thick.

Bake for 15 minutes until just lightly golden. Switch off the oven and leave the door slightly ajar, and place the macaroons on the bottom of the oven to allow them to dry completely,

makes 15 to 20

115 g/4 oz/½ cup ground hazelnuts
50 g/2 oz/½ cup caster sugar
50 g/2 oz/½ cup lavender sugar – see p.20
1 egg white

for 15 to 20 minutes. Remove and allow to cool on the baking sheet, before serving, or, when absolutely cold, storing in an airtight container. These make a perfect accompaniment to lavender ice-cream.

Lavender brownies

This is a very easy recipe which children enjoy making. The lavender is a perfect match for the chocolate.

Melt the chocolate and butter in a bowl set over hot water. Beat in the sugar and eggs. Stir in the flour and salt until well-mixed than add the nuts. Bake in a greased 20 cm/8 inch square pan and bake for 30 to 35 minutes at 180°C/350°F/ gas mark 4 until the top has a dull crust. It will give slightly if you touch it with your finger. Cool slightly then cut into squares and carefully lift out of the pan with a spatula to cool further on a wire rack.

makes 10 to 12

75 g/3 oz dark chocolate – at least 70% cocoa solids
75 g/3 oz/¾ stick butter
75 g/3 oz/⅓ cup caster sugar
50 g/2 oz/¼ cup lavender sugar – see p.20
2 eggs, *beaten with*
1 or 2 drops culinary lavender essence
115 g/4 oz/1 cup self-raising flour
a pinch of salt
50 g/2 oz/½ cup chopped walnuts

Lavender honey cake

Similar to German *Lebkuchen*, this glazed, spiced biscuit-type cake should be kept for several days before cutting, as it is crisp and hard when first baked and then becomes softer and chewier. You can also bake individual cakes, heaping teaspoons or soupspoons of the mixture on the baking sheet and flattening slightly with a damp spoon.

Grease or line a baking sheet.

serves 6 to 8

150 g/5 oz/⅔ cup caster sugar
1 egg
75 g/3 oz/⅓ cup lavender sugar – see p.20
150 g/6 oz/½ cup lavender honey

Beat the sugar and egg together. Put the lavender sugar and honey in a saucepan with the water and heat until the sugar has dissolved. Pour it into a large bowl and add the egg and sugar mixture. Beat well. Fold in the rest of the ingredients until well mixed. Roll out to a 1 cm/½ inch thick round on a very lightly floured worktop. Carefully place on the baking sheet and bake for 20 minutes at 220°C/425°F/gas mark 7. When cool, cover very thinly with water icing (see p.24), lightly perfumed with a drop of culinary lavender essence.

1 tablespoon water
225 g/8 oz/2 cups self-raising flour
50 g/2 oz/⅓ cup ground almonds
50 g/2 oz/½ cup chopped almonds
1 tablespoon chopped candied lemon peel
½ teaspoon ground cardamom

Rose petal fancies

Grease or line a baking sheet.

Sift the flour and ground rice and rub in the butter. Add the sugar and the egg, together with the rose essence and colouring, if using it. Mix well to a stiff paste. Divide into small balls and make a hollow in the middle of each. Spoon in a little rose petal jelly. Place on the baking sheet. Flatten slightly and brush with the reserved egg white. Bake at 200°C/400°F/gas mark 6 until golden brown for about 15 minutes. Cool on a wire rack.

makes about 20 buns

175 g/6 oz/1 ½ cups self-raising flour
150 g/6 oz/1 cup ground rice
115 g/4 oz/1 stick unsalted butter
115 g/4 oz/½ cup caster sugar
2 egg yolks, *beaten with*
1 tablespoon rosewater
a drop of rose essence
pink or red food colouring – optional
rose petal jelly – see p.22
1 egg white

Macarons à la rose, rose and almond macaroons

As with all meringue-style preparations, do not attempt these in humid conditions.

Line baking sheets with silicone.

Sift the ground almonds and measured sugar together. This must be absolutely smooth and fine. Whisk the egg whites and, as they firm up, sprinkle in the powdered egg white and the extra tablespoon of sifted icing sugar, together with the food colouring and essence, only a drop, mind, whisking until the mixture is very firm, smooth and glossy. Add some of the almond and sugar mixture to the egg white and fold in gently, and then gently fold in the remaining dry ingredients, which should finish with the consistency of soft paste and remain glossy and smooth.

Pipe into small rounds, about 2.5 cm/1 inch apart, on the baking sheet and let the *macarons* dry for about an hour. Bang the tray to remove any air bubbles and bake at 180°C/350°F/ gas mark 4 for 8 minutes. Turn the tray around and cook for another 7 minutes. Remove from the oven and carefully transfer to a wire rack to cool. When cold, sandwich pairs of *macarons* with jelly or jam and rose butter cream.

makes about 20

150 g/5 oz/1 cup ground almonds
225 g/8 oz/1⅔ cups icing sugar, plus 1 tablespoon, well-sifted
4 or 5 egg whites (from 4 or 5 eggs)
a drop of red or pink food colouring
a drop of culinary rose essence – see pp.14 and 15
1 teaspoon dried egg white powder, optional – see recipe

Filling

rose petal jelly – see p.22 – or jam
rose butter cream (see over)

Rose butter cream

Mix all the ingredients until you have a smooth mass. Store in an airtight container in the refrigerator until ready to use, then allow to come to room temperature.

50 g/2 oz/½ stick unsalted butter, softened but not oily
50 g/2 oz/scant ½ cup icing sugar
2 tablespoons rosewater
a drop or two of pink or red food colouring

Orange flower *macarons*

Inspired by the eighteenth-century cooks and their flower water recipes, this is nevertheless a modern recipe for the classic French *macaron*, which I was taught to make by a French *pâtissier* some years ago. Floral flavours and fillings are almost infinite. Try violet flavouring for a macaron with a blackcurrant filling or the palest green pistachio *macaron* filled with a buttercream scented with elderflower syrup or jasmine jelly (see p.22).

Line baking sheets with silicone.

Sift the ground almonds and measured sugar together. This must be absolutely smooth and fine. Whisk the egg whites and, as they firm up, sprinkle in the powdered egg white and the tablespoon of sugar, whisking until the mixture is very firm, smooth and glossy. Add some of the almond and sugar mixture to the egg white and fold in gently, then gently fold in the remaining dry ingredients and the orange zest. The mixture should have the consistency of soft paste and remain glossy and smooth.

makes about 40

150 g/5 oz/1 cup ground almonds
225 g/8 oz/1 ⅓ cups icing sugar, plus 1 tablespoon
115 ml/4 fl oz/just over ½ cup egg whites (from 4 or 5 eggs)
1 tsp dried egg white powder – optional
2 teaspoons very finely grated orange zest
a drop of orange food colouring

Pipe into small mounds, about 2.5 cm/1 inch apart, on baking sheets lined with non-stick baking material. Let the macaroons dry in a warm place for an hour before baking at 180°C/350°F/gas mark 3 for 8 minutes. Turn the tray around and cook for another 7 minutes.

Allow to cool, then sandwich with the following mixture.

Orange flower cream

Whisk all the ingredients together until just firm enough to use as a filling. This is also an excellent filling for sponge cakes.

225 ml/8 fl oz/1 cup double cream
1 tablespoon finely grated orange zest
2 tablespoons icing sugar
2 tablespoons orange flower water

Rose meringues

Rose petal meringues are the perfect base for that exquisite summer dessert, Eton Mess, simply crushing the meringues and mixing with strawberries and whipped cream, which can also be scented with a hint of rosewater.

Line a baking sheet with non-stick baking parchment or a silicone mat.

Put the egg white in a scrupulously clean bowl – any film of grease will prevent it attaining its full volume. Sprinkle on a tablespoon of sugar and begin whisking. When the egg white is foamy and increased in volume, add half the remaining sugar and continue whisking.

makes 4

1 large egg white
100 g/scant 4 oz/scant ½ cup rose petal sugar – see p.20

The meringue will begin to take shape, becoming glossy and with smaller bubbles. Continue whisking until you have added all the sugar and the meringue is now a firm mass of glossy foam, with tiny bubbles.

When you trail the whisk through it, the mixture will peak and hold its shape.

Spoon or pipe the meringue into four heaps and bake, or rather, dry, in a preheated oven at 125–150°C/250–275°F/gas mark ½–1 for about 45 minutes. Cool on a wire rack and store in an airtight tin until required.

Cook's tip

Quantities can be increased by simple multiplication. For filled meringues, pipe or spoon into heaps on the baking sheet and, when cooked and cooled, sandwich with whipped cream flavoured with a splash of rosewater or rose essence, delicately tinted with pink food colouring if you wish.

Lavender chocolate meringues

Grease and flour or line two baking sheets.

Sift the icing sugar and cocoa. Whisk the egg whites to firm peaks, adding a tablespoon of lavender sugar after a minute or two. When the whites are firm, gently whisk in the remaining sugar and then carefully fold in the cocoa mixture. Spoon the meringue mixture onto the baking trays in neat ovals, using two tablespoons to shape it. Bake in a preheated oven at 150°C/300°F/gas mark 2 for about an hour. Take care that the meringues do not brown. Turn the baking sheets to ensure regular baking. When the meringues are

makes 6 to 8

This recipe contains uncooked eggs

Meringue

50 g/2 oz/scant ½ cup icing sugar
1 tablespoon cocoa powder
2 egg whites
50 g/2 oz/½ cup lavender sugar made with caster sugar – see p.20

cooked, remove them from the oven and allow to cool and dry out.

Melt the chocolate in a bowl set over hot water. Remove from the heat and, when cooled slightly, beat in the butter until smoothly incorporated. Thoroughly mix in the egg yolks and essence, and, when the mixture is cool, whisk the egg whites and gently fold in the chocolate mixture. Use this mousse to sandwich two meringues together.

Mousse

150 g/5 oz dark chocolate –
    at least 70% solids
25 g/1 oz/¼ stick unsalted
    butter, softened and at
    room temperature
2 eggs, separated
a drop or two of culinary
    lavender essence

Lavender almond crisps

These are perfect accompaniments to ice-creams, sorbets, mousses and custards, and indeed, with a cup of tea or coffee.

Line two baking sheets with rice paper or silicone. Mix together the dry ingredients, and then fold in the egg whites until thoroughly blended. The mixture can be piped or spooned onto the baking trays. Leave plenty of room for the mixture to spread.

Bake at 180°C/350°F/gas mark 4 for 20 minutes or until a pale golden brown. Cool on a wire rack.

makes 24

115 g/4 oz/⅔ cup ground
    almonds
1 tablespoon rice flour
115 g/4 oz/½ cup caster
    sugar
115 g/4 oz/½ cup lavender
    sugar – see p.20
1 teaspoon five-spice powder
2 egg whites, lightly whisked

Rose and coconut macaroons

These sweetmeats are very easy to make, something that children might enjoy helping with.

Line a baking sheet with rice paper.

Mix the coconut and sugar, add a little rosewater and enough egg white to bind

makes about 20

115 g/4 oz/1 cup desiccated
    coconut
50 g/2 oz/¼ cup rose petal
    sugar – see p.20
50 g/2 oz/¼ cup caster
    sugar

together in a firm paste. Use two teaspoons, dipped in water, to shape small oval lozenges. Place them on the baking sheet and bake in a preheated oven at 160°C/325°F/gas mark 3 for about 15 to 20 minutes, until just pale gold. Remove from the oven, top each with a piece of crystallised rose petal and cool on a wire rack.

rosewater – see recipe
egg white – see recipe
crystallised rose petals – see
  p.19

Almond hearts

These make excellent sweetmeats with an after-dinner coffee or tisane.

Line a baking sheet with rice paper or silicone.

Mix the almonds and icing sugar, and add the orange flower water and zest. Mix in just enough egg white to bind together to a firm paste that can be rolled out. It is easy to over-do the egg white, and you will find yourself adding extra ground almond to 'dry' the mixture.

Wrap in cling film and chill for an hour. Roll out to about 1 cm/½ inch thick, dusting the worktop and rolling pin with cornflour if necessary to stop the mixture sticking.

Cut with a heart-shaped cutter, place on a baking sheet, lined with rice paper, and bake in a preheated oven at 160°C/325°F/gas mark 3 for 15 to 20 minutes, until pale gold. Cool on a wire rack and sift icing sugar over them before serving.

makes about 30

115 g/4 oz/⅔ cup ground
  almonds
115 g/4 oz/¾ cup icing
  sugar, sifted
1 teaspoon orange flower
  water
2 teaspoons grated orange or
  mandarin zest
egg white – see recipe

Variations

Use rosewater and decorate with crystallised rose petals, or violet essence and crystallised violets – see p.19.

Rose petal éclairs

You can adapt this recipe to any of the floral flavours; a lavender water ice with a chocolate lavender custard filling is very good, as is the reverse, a chocolate topping with a lavender custard filling. The chocolate icing is simply melted chocolate. White chocolate and violet is another perfect combination.

Grease and flour or line two baking sheets with silicone or baking parchment.

Bring the milk, butter, sugar and salt to the boil in a saucepan. Add the flour in one go and mix it vigorously until it leaves the sides of the pan. Remove from the heat. After a few minutes, when the mixture has cooled somewhat, beat in the eggs, one at a time. Spoon the paste into an icing bag with a round nozzle. Pipe 18 lengths onto the prepared sheets, well spaced out. Bake for 20 to 25 minutes at 190°C/375°F/gas mark 5, until light golden brown. Transfer to a wire rack to cool.

In a bowl beat the egg yolks with the sugar and syrup and blend in the flour. Bring the milk to the boil and pour it onto the egg and flour mixture, whisking continuously. Transfer to a saucepan and let it thicken over a low heat, stirring all the while for about 5 minutes. Once slightly cooled, cover the custard with cling film and refrigerate for a couple of hours.

Spoon the custard into a piping bag. Make a small hole in the base of each éclair and fill with the rose-scented custard, or simply split them and fill that way.

makes 18

225 ml/8 fl oz/1 cup semi-skimmed milk
115 g/4 oz/1 stick unsalted butter
50 g/2 oz/¼ cup caster sugar
½ coffeespoon salt
150 g/5 oz/1¼ cup plain flour
4 eggs

For the filling

4 egg yolks
115 g/4 oz/½ cup rose petal sugar – see p.20
3 tablespoons rose petal syrup – see p.23
80 g/3½ oz/⅞ cup plain flour
600 ml/20 fl oz/2½ cups whole milk

For the decoration

225 g/8 oz/1⅔ cups icing sugar
a drop or two of pink food colouring
a drop or two of culinary rose essence
lemon juice – see recipe
18 crystallised rose petals or pieces – see p.19

Make a soft icing by sifting the icing sugar into a bowl and mixing with food colouring, rose essence and enough lemon juice to make a soft but not runny icing. Spread it quickly and smoothly over the top of the éclair.

Cook's tip

As an easy alternative to the custard, a simple whipped cream scented with rose petal syrup can be made.

Saffron and Cheddar puff with goats' cheese, chive and floral confetti filling

Based on the traditional *gougère* so often served when one tours the wine cellars of Chablis, this is made with English, not to say West Country, flavours.

Lightly grease a baking sheet.

Bring the water, butter and salt to the boil in a medium-sized saucepan and, when it does so, tip in all the flour at once, stirring vigorously with a wooden spoon. As you stir, the mixture will dry and become smooth to the point where it leaves the sides of the pan. Remove from the heat and beat in the eggs, a little at a time, making sure each addition is thoroughly incorporated. Because the absorbent quality of flour can change from batch to batch and can vary with the day's humidity, it is a good idea not to add the whole of the second egg, as you may not need it all to give you a soft, pliable but not liquid dough. On the other hand, if the flour is very dry, you may need to add a little more beaten egg. At this point, too, add the Cheddar and the saffron and its liquid. Keep stirring until you have a smooth paste.

makes 1 large choux ring

115 ml/4 fl oz/½ cup water
2 oz/50 g/½ stick butter
a pinch of salt
75 g/3 oz/¾ cup plain flour
2 eggs, lightly beaten
115 g/4 oz/1 cup Cheddar, grated
¹/₂₀ g/25 saffron threads soaked in 1 tablespoon boiling water

Filling

175 g/6 oz soft fresh goats' cheese, rind removed
2 tablespoons chopped chives
50 g/2 oz/²/₃ cup floral confetti – see cook's note below
freshly ground black pepper

The mixture can be kept now for use later. If you wish to do this, cover the surface with damp greaseproof paper to stop a crust forming. Otherwise, proceed immediately.

The oven should be preheated to 180°C/ 350°F/gas mark 4. Spoon the paste into a round, about 20 cm/8 inches in diameter, on the baking sheet. Bake for about 25 to 30 minutes. Turn off the heat and allow to cool with the oven door open. While the pastry is cooling, prepare the filling.

Break up the goats' cheese and mix in a bowl until smooth. Season with pepper, stir in the chives, and carefully fold in the flower confetti. Split the cheese puff and spread with the filling. Cut into wedges to serve.

Cook's note on flower confetti

Flower confetti is exactly what it says. Indeed, you can make it to throw over a bridal couple as well as use it in the kitchen. To make it, you need flower petals of roughly the same size, or petals that can be rolled and sliced with a sharp knife to produce shredded petals. Smaller petals can be used whole.

This is, of course, less about the flavour of flowers and more about their appearance and how to use them other than simply strewing them over salads. It is so pretty and effective that you will find many uses for it.

The flower petals are best used within an hour or so of being gathered, laying the petals on a damp tea towel until required. Or you can dry them and store them, but they will lose some of their colour. However, dried floral confetti is effective in scones and muffins, both sweet and savoury.

Bergamot, borage, chrysanthemum, cornflower, daisy and marigold petals, nasturtium flowers, wild rose petals all make a splendid confetti, but, as with any flowers used in the kitchen, make sure they come from unsprayed cultivation.

For the savoury goats' cheese filling, I like to use nasturtiums, marigolds and cornflowers.

Wild garlic flower and cheese popovers

Batter rather than choux paste is the base for these popovers, which are similar to Yorkshire puddings in preparation and baking, as well as in the end result. The wild garlic, a spring-time treat, adds not the fragrance of rose or lavender, but a punchy savoury quality that makes these crisp yet tender morsels the perfect accompaniment to drinks. Strip the flower heads from the stems and then chop these as you would chives.

It is important not to use too strong a cheese; a mature cheddar or Parmesan will overwhelm the subtle flavour of the wild garlic. I prefer to use a crumbly Lancashire or a young Cantal. A hard English goats' cheese, such as Swaledale or St Helen's, works perfectly.

Beat the flour, egg and enough water together to make a smooth batter and stir in the crumbled or grated cheese, wild garlic flowers and chopped stalks. Lightly butter bun tins and pour in the batter. Bake in a preheated oven at 200°C/400°F/gas mark 6 for 15 to 18 minutes. They should be golden brown and puffed up when cooked, though will sink somewhat when removed from the oven. Serve as hot as possible.

makes 12

75 g/3 oz/¾ cup plain flour

2 eggs

up to 200 ml/7 fl oz/⅞ cup water

115 g/4 oz/1 cup cheese – see recipe

12 to 15 stems of wild garlic flowers

butter – see recipe

Tarts, pies and pastries

Mainly sweet, but including savoury onion and wild garlic tarts, the recipes here are versatile. You can adapt a recipe for a large tart and use it for individual tarts or tartlets, and vice versa. Jam tarts and lemon curd tarts played a large part in my childhood kichen experiences, but then disappeared from my repertoire in favour of more sophisticated baking. With exquisite pastry, incorporating flower petals or flower sugar and a delicately hued and flavoured filling, the jam tart deserves to be rehabilitated and take its place at elegant afternoon teas alongside cup cakes, macaroons, éclairs and all the other fashionable pastries.

"I like the tropical flavours here, the highly scented jasmine beneath the light coconut sponge."

Jasmine and coconut tarts, p.129

Basic pastry recipes

Short crust pastry

Sift the flour and salt together in a bowl. Cut in the butter and then, with your fingertips, rub the mixture lightly together, lifting it to incorporate plenty of air, until it resembles breadcrumbs. Use a palette knife to mix in enough water to bind the mixture to a dough.

225 g/8 oz/2 cups plain flour
1 scant teaspoon salt
115 g/4 oz/1 stick unsalted butter, chilled and diced
about 6 tablespoons chilled water

Work it into a ball. Cover and chill the pastry for 30 minutes. Flour the worktop and lightly roll out the pastry as required.

Sweet short crust pastry

Rub the flour and butter together until well combined and crumbly, but do not overwork. Stir in the salt and sugar, and then the egg and enough iced water to bind. Wrap and cool in the refrigerator for 20 minutes before using.

225 g/8 oz/1 cup plain flour
115 g/4 oz/1 stick unsalted butter, chilled and diced
a pinch of salt
50 g/2 oz/¼ cup caster sugar
1 small egg, lightly beaten
iced water – see recipe

Flaky pastry

Make the pastry as for short pastry above, using only half the butter. After it has been chilled for 30 minutes, roll the dough into a rectangle, with the short sides top and bottom. Dot half the remaining butter over the bottom two-thirds of the dough. Fold the top third down and the bottom third over it. Press to seal the sides. Give a quarter turn and roll out again to the same rectangular shape you started with. Fold it into three as before, without the butter; give it another quarter turn and roll out into another rectangle. Dot with the rest of the butter, fold the dough as before, give it a turn, roll it and continue with two more turns.

If the kitchen or your hands are getting too warm, chill the dough in the refrigerator before continuing. After the last turn, roll the dough as required.

225 g/8 oz/2 cups plain flour
scant teaspoon salt
115 g/4 oz/1 stick unsalted butter, chilled and diced
about 6 tablespoons chilled water

Each of the three basic pastry recipes will make eighteen 6 cm/2½ inch tarts or twelve 8 cm/3 inch tarts, and will line a 22–25 cm/ 9–10 inch flan dish

Puff pastry

I'm not ashamed to admit that I buy all-butter
puff pastry. For Shirley Conran life is too short
to stuff a mushroom. For me, life is too short
to make puff pastry.

To bake blind

Roll out the pastry and line a greased tart
tin (20 to 25 cm/8 to 10 inches in diameter).
Prick the pastry all over, line with greaseproof
paper, weight down with ceramic baking
beans (dried beans will do, and can be stored
and re-used for the same purpose) and bake
blind – that is, empty – for 10 to 12 minutes in
a preheated oven at 200°C/400°/gas mark 6.

Remove from the oven, take out the beans and
paper, and let the pastry case cool.

Saffron and onion tart

Rub the flour and butter together until it
resembles breadcrumbs and stir in enough
water to bind the pastry together. Wrap and
refrigerate while you make the onion filling.

I have based this recipe on the traditional
Alsace dish, but have added saffron, which
lends lovely warm notes and fragrance. The
tart takes a good deal more time and patience
than its cousin the *quiche lorraine*. The onions
must be cooked very slowly to achieve a
translucent melting texture and a sweet flavour
without the caramelisation that comes from
too high a heat. Look for mild, sweet onions.

serves 6 or 8

For the pastry case

225 g/8 oz/2 cups plain flour
115 g/4 oz/1 stick butter, cut
   into small cubes
about 75 ml/3 fl oz/⅓ cup
   iced water

Freshly dug bulbs can be used; indeed, in spring in Alsace they make a version with spring onions, adding some of the green tops.

The best *zewelwai* I have tasted was in the Caveau d'Eguisheim, a restaurant started by Léon Beyer, father of one of the present-day wine makers, as a showcase for Alsace food and wine. *Vignerons* who bought a share in it were able to put their wines on the list, and they were sold at very reasonable prices in the restaurant. We drank a 1985 Riesling with the tart. I remember its flinty crispness as a perfect foil for the mellow suavity of the onions.

Melt the butter in a heavy frying pan and gently fry the onions until they start to turn soft, translucent and are just beginning to change colour. Remove from the heat, sprinkle on the flour and gradually stir in the saffron and liquid and the cream. Bring to the boil, stirring continuously, and cook for five minutes. Season with salt and pepper, and grind in a little fresh nutmeg. Beat in the eggs, one at a time, away from the heat.

Line a 25 cm/10 inch quiche or pie dish with pastry and pour in the filling. Place the dish on a baking sheet in a preheated oven, 200°C/400°F/gas mark 6, for about 35 minutes, until the top is golden brown. The tart can be served at any temperature, but I prefer it warm.

For the filling

1/20 g/25 saffron threads, soaked in 2 tablespoons boiling water
115 g/4 oz/1 stick butter
6 mild onions, peeled and thinly sliced
1 tablespoon flour
300 ml/10 fl oz/1 ¼ cups single cream or full-cream milk
salt
pepper
freshly grated nutmeg
3 eggs

Wild garlic flower and cream cheese tart

This is a recipe to make when you have left-over egg whites. I have based it on a sweet medieval recipe for sambocade, which was made with elderflowers. Here the tart is savoury using wild garlic flowers. Egg whites alone keep the tart filling elegantly pale. It would be a perfect vegetarian first course for a spring lunch when wild garlic flowers are in bloom. To prepare the flowers, separate the flower heads and chop the stems as you would for chives; both parts are used.

Use a mild cheese such as Lancashire, young Cantal or Edam rather than Cheddar or Parmesan, which will overpower the subtle flavour of the wild garlic.

Grease and flour a 25 cm/10 inch tart tin.

Mix the cheeses and cream until soft and well-blended. Beat in two of the egg whites. Whisk the other two egg whites and fold into the creamed mixture, together with the wild garlic flowers and stems.

Spoon the cream into the pastry case, tap it hard on the worktop to settle the mixture and bake in a moderate oven, about 160°C/325°F/ gas mark 3 for about 25 to 30 minutes, until the mixture has just set. It is important not to use a higher heat, as this will set the protein in the egg white much too firmly and cause the tarts to brown too much; they should remain pale and delicate in appearance.

serves 4 to 6

300 g/10 oz plain short crust pastry – see p.119
225 g/8 oz/1 ⅓ cups cream cheese
50 g/2 oz/½ cup crumbled or grated mild cheese – see recipe
75 ml/3 fl oz/⅓ cup double cream
4 egg whites
about 2 dozen stems of wild garlic flowers

Tomato and lavender tart

I wrote in *The Scented Kitchen* about the 'androgynous' nature of lavender, a flower which marries sweet or savoury equally well. It is excellent with tomatoes, themselves somewhat androgynous – fruit, but treated as a vegetable. Here the lavender is every bit as effective as the more usual partners for tomatoes, basil or mint, and that bit more unusual. It makes an exquisite vegetarian first course for a summer meal.

Working on a floured worktop, roll the pastry to fit an oiled shallow tart tin about 25 cm/ 10 inches in diameter, or simply roll it free-form and place on an oiled baking sheet.

Arrange the tomato slices on top, in overlapping circles, and brush with the remaining oil. Sprinkle on the lavender flowers and lightly season with salt and pepper. Bake in the top half of a preheated oven at 200°C/400°F/ gas mark 6, for 20 to 25 minutes. This tastes best warm, or at room temperature, but not refrigerated.

Cook's tip

If you can bear to skin the tomatoes first, the tart will be even more elegant, as well as easier to eat. Small tomatoes, such as miniature plum or cherry tomatoes, halved and placed dome-side up, also work well here.

serves 4 to 6

300 g/10 oz short crust pastry – see p.119
4 tablespoons extra virgin olive oil
6 cloves garlic, peeled and thinly sliced – optional
750 g/1 ½ lb firm, ripe tomatoes, sliced
1 teaspoon chopped lavender flowers
sea salt
freshly ground black pepper

Mqaret

Maqrut means lozenge-shaped in Arabic, from which much of the Maltese language developed, just as many of the islands' desserts and pastries have Arab origins. *Mqaret* is a good example, a deep-fried pastry lozenge with a rich filling of dates scented with anis and orange flower water. You can also bake them, in which case they are a perfect winter teatime treat, or, in miniature versions, as *petits fours*. They are served at Ta' Frenc restaurant on Gozo as part of a Maltese dessert platter.

Line or grease and flour a baking sheet.

Make the filling first, as it needs to cool before you use it. Put the chopped dates in a saucepan with a couple of tablespoons of water. Cook for several minutes until the dates have softened. Remove from the heat and stir in the rest of the ingredients. Allow to cool while you make the pastry.

Because I bake them, I make a rather richer pastry than if I were frying them, doubling the quantity of butter. Rub the flour and most of the butter together with your fingertips, lifting it to incorporate plenty of air, until it resembles breadcrumbs. Using a palette knife, mix in the orange flower and enough water to bind the mixture to a dough. Work it into a ball. Cover and chill the pastry for 30 minutes.

Divide the pastry in half as it is easier to work with. Roll the first piece out to a 10 x 40 cm/ 4 x 16 inch rectangle. Take half the filling and spoon in down one long side of the pastry, leaving a 1 cm/½ inch border. Brush this with water. Fold the pastry over to enclose

makes 16

Filling

225 g/8 oz/2 cups dates, stoned and chopped

grated zest of 1 tangerine or mandarin

a pinch of ground cloves

½ teaspoon dried fennel flower

1 tablespoon orange flower water

1 tablespoon anis liqueur (pastis or ouzo will do very well, if you don't have Maltese anis liqueur)

1 tablespoon icing sugar

Pastry

225 g/8 oz/2 cups plain flour

115 g/4 oz/1 stick butter plus extra for glazing

1 tablespoon orange flower water

1 tbsp water

the filling and seal the edge well. Cut into 8 lozenge shapes and place on the baking sheet. Prepare the second piece of pastry and filling in the same way. Chill the pastries for 20 to 30 minutes. Melt the remaining butter and brush over the pastries before baking them for 15 to 20 minutes at 190°C/375°F/gas mark 5 until a rich golden brown. Transfer to a wire rack to cool and serve warm or room temperature, dusting with icing sugar before serving.

Rose and almond meringue slices

This is based on a recipe from the 1950s teatime repertoire, and is just as good today.

Line or grease and flour a baking sheet.

Roll out the pastry to a 22 x 15 cm/9 x 6 inch rectangle and place on the baking sheet. Spread with the jam or jelly and bake for 10 minutes in a preheated oven at 180°C/350°F/gas mark 4 for 12 minutes. Make meringue by whisking the egg whites to firm peaks with 1 tablespoon sugar, then gradually folding in the remaining sugar, whisking continuously until you have a firm, glossy mass. Fold in the almonds. When the pastry is cooked, spread meringue over the top and bake at 160–180°C/325–350°F/ gas mark 3–4 until the meringue is pale brown. Cool on a wire rack and cut into rectangles to serve.

makes 6 to 8 slices

175 g/6 oz short crust pastry
 – see p.119
rose petal jam or jelly – see
 p.22
2 egg whites
50 g/2 oz/¼ cup rose petal
 sugar, finely ground – see
 p.20
25 g/1 oz/2 tablespoons
 chopped almonds

Cook's tip

If you have no rose petal sugar, put a few crystallised rose petals with granulated sugar and grind until fine.

Orange and almond pastries

I like to serve these small almond pastries, to which marmalade gives a hint of bitterness, with tiny cups of espresso or thick Spanish hot chocolate.

Rub the flour and butter together until well combined and crumbly, but do not overwork. Stir in the salt, sugar and orange zest, and then the egg with enough iced water to bind. Wrap and cool in the refrigerator for 20 minutes before using.

Mix the ingredients for the filling. Roll the pastry and cut out into 7.5 cm/3 inch circles, and put a teaspoon of the filling on each half. Fold over the pastries, having first dampened the edges, and seal them well. Bake in a preheated oven at 200°C/400°F/gas mark 6 for 10 minutes, then turn down a notch and bake for further 5 to 10 minutes. Serve warm or cold, dusted with icing sugar.

makes 18 to 20

Pastry

225 g/8 oz/1 cup plain flour
115 g/4 oz/1 stick unsalted butter, chilled and diced
a pinch of salt
50 g/2 oz/¼ cup caster sugar
grated zest of 1 orange or tangerine
1 small egg, *lightly beaten with*
1 tablespoon orange flower water
iced water – see recipe

Filling

115 g/4 oz/⅔ cup ground almonds
115 g/4 oz/½ cup caster sugar
2 tablespoons tangerine or orange marmalade with the peel chopped very fine
1 to 2 teaspoons orange flower water
2 tablespoons unsalted butter, melted

Lavender walnut fancy

This is a rather elegant teatime pastry, which can also be served warm as a dessert.

Line or grease and flour a 20 cm/8 inch square cake tin.

Rub the butter into the flour, add the sugars, stir in the egg yolks and enough milk to make a firm pastry-like dough. Roll out to fit the cake tin. For the topping, whisk the egg white until firm, gradually adding the sugar and the lavender essence. Fold in the nuts and spread over the pastry. Bake at 180°C/350°F/gas mark 4 for 20 to 25 minutes. Allow to cool slightly in the pan, then cut into portions and carefully lift out the pieces to cool on a wire rack.

makes 16 squares

75 g/3 oz/¾ stick unsalted butter

175 g/6 oz/1 ½ cups self-raising flour

50 g/2 oz/¼ cup caster sugar

1 tablespoon lavender sugar – see p.20

2 egg yolks, *lightly beaten with*

2 drops culinary lavender essence

milk – see recipe

Topping

2 egg whites

75 g/3 oz/⅓ cup caster sugar

a drop of lavender culinary essence

50 g/2 oz/½ cup walnuts, chopped

50 g/2 oz/½ cup toasted and skinned hazelnuts, chopped

grated zest of half a lemon

Jasmine and coconut tarts

I like the tropical flavours here, the highly scented jasmine beneath the light coconut sponge.

Grease and flour twelve 8 cm/3 inch bun tins

Roll out the pastry on a floured worktop, cut into rounds and fit them into the bun tins. Place half a teaspoon of jasmine jelly in each. Cream the butter and sugar. Stir in the desiccated coconut and 1 beaten egg. Use a teaspoon to shape the mixture into 24 balls and place one in each case, flattening slightly. Bake at 180–190°C/350–375°F/gas mark 4–5 for about 15 minutes. You can brush these with more jasmine jelly while still warm and decorate with a crystallised jasmine flower. Use the same recipe as the basis for making rose and almond tarts.

makes 12

225 g/8 oz short crust pastry – see p.119
2 tablespoons jasmine jelly – see p.22
115 g/4 oz/1 stick butter
115 g/4 oz/½ cup caster sugar
115 g/4 oz/⅔ cup desiccated coconut
1 egg, lightly beaten

Elderflower tarts

A custard recipe (see p.115) always leaves you with far more egg whites than you know what to do with. Here is a lovely elderflower recipe, based on the medieval sambocade, which makes the most of them. Using egg whites alone keeps the filling of the tarts elegantly pale. These would be perfect for a celebration tea in late spring when the elder tree is in full blossom.

Grease and flour twelve 8 cm/3 inch or eighteen 6 cm/2½ inch tartlet tins.

Cream the cheese and sugar until soft, then stir in the syrup and cream until well blended. Beat in two of the egg whites. Whisk the other

makes 12 to 18

225 g/8 oz sweet short crust pastry – see p.120
225 g/8 oz/1 ⅓ cups cream cheese or mascarpone
50 g/2 oz/½ cup caster sugar
1 tablespoon elderflower syrup
75 ml/3 fl oz/⅓ cup double cream
4 egg whites
6–8 elderflower heads, flowers only

two egg whites and fold into the creamed mixture, together with the elderflowers.

Spoon the cream into the pastry case, tap it hard on the worktop to settle the mixture, and bake in a moderate oven, about 160°C/325°F/ gas mark 3 for about 15 to 20 minutes, until the mixture has just set. It is important not to use a higher heat, as this will set the protein in the egg white much too firmly and cause the tarts to brown too much; they should remain pale and delicate in appearance.

Double chocolate and lavender tarts

Rub the butter into the flour and cocoa and then stir in the sugar and egg yolk. Add iced water, if necessary, to bind to a pastry. Leave it to rest for half an hour, then roll out and line twelve 6 cm/2½ inch pastry cases.

Bake blind for 6 to 8 minutes, remove from the oven and leave to cool. You can make these a day or so in advance, if you wish.

Whisk the eggs and sugar until pale and much increased in volume. In a bowl set over a pan of hot water, melt the chocolate in the cream. Remove from the heat, beat in the butter and fold into the egg mixture.

Leave to cool, then spoon into the pastry cases and bake at 150°C/300°F/gas mark 2 in a preheated oven for 5 minutes.

Cool on a wire rack before serving, dusted with icing sugar and decorated with some frosted lavender flowers.

makes 12

Pastry

50 g/2 oz/½ stick unsalted butter

75 g/3 oz/¾ cup plain flour, *sifted with*

2 tablespoons cocoa

1 tablespoon caster sugar

1 egg yolk

iced water

Filling

1 egg plus 2 yolks

50 g/2 oz/¼ cup lavender sugar – see p.20

50 ml/2 fl oz/¼ cup double cream

150 g/5 oz dark chocolate, at least 70% cocoa solids, broken

25 g/1 oz/¼ stick unsalted butter, softened

Lavender and lemon cheesecakes

Based on traditional English cheesecake recipes, such as Maids of Honour, there is no cheese in the recipe, but the lemon juice curdles the cream, giving the same effect.

Butter and flour 2 trays of tartlet moulds.

Line the tart cases with the pastry. Mix the rest of the ingredients in the order given, making sure that everything is thoroughly blended before adding the cream. Spoon into the pastry cases and bake for 15 to 20 minutes in a preheated oven at 180°C/350°F/gas mark 4. Remove and cool on wire racks.

makes 24 tartlets

225 g/8 oz sweet short crust pastry – see p.120
115 g/4 oz/²⁄₃ cup ground almonds
3 egg yolks
25 g/1 oz/1 tablespoon lavender sugar – see p.20
25 g/1 oz/1 tablespoon caster sugar
50 g/2 oz/½ stick unsalted butter, melted
grated zest and juice of 1 large lemon
150 ml/5 fl oz/⅝ cup double cream

Lavender *mille-feuilles*

Napoleons and vanilla slices are other names for the original pastry on which my recipe is based. Crisp puff pastry is split and spread with lavender pastry cream. Traditionally, the water ice topping is feathered with chocolate icing, but here I would use a little of the water icing tinted a darker purple, or use a gel pen.

First, make the pastry cream. Pour the milk into a saucepan, bring it to the boil and beat in the sugar, cornstarch, and eggs. Put the saucepan back on medium heat while stirring constantly with a wire whisk until the custard starts to thicken. Remove from the heat, whisk once more and allow to cool. When the custard is almost cold, stir in the lavender

makes 8

Lavender pastry cream

225 ml/8 fl oz/1 cup milk
1 egg plus 2 yolks, lightly beaten
50 g/2 oz/¼ cup sugar
25 g/1 oz/3 tablespoons cornflour
115 ml/4 oz/½ cup double cream
2 drops culinary lavender essence, to taste – see p.14

essence. Whip the cream and carefully fold it into the custard with a palette knife. Cover and keep in the fridge until ready to use.

Unroll the pastry and cut into evenly-sized rectangles. Place on a lined or greased and floured baking sheet and bake in a preheated oven at about 220°C/450°F/gas mark 6 for 15 minutes or so until puffed up and golden.

Transfer to a wire rack and, when cool, split the pastry through the centre. Brush lavender jelly on one half, then carefully spread the pastry cream over it. Top with the other half of pastry. To decorate the pastries, mix the sugar and lemon juice to the required texture, add the colouring if using it, and the lavender essence. Spread it quickly over the top of the pastries.

1 pack bought puff pastry, already rolled
lavender jelly – see p.21

Glacé icing

icing sugar, sifted
lemon juice, strained
a drop of food colouring, optional
a drop or two of culinary floral essence

Lemon and lavender pie

Using the same method as the traditional Key lime pie – biscuit crust and condensed milk filling – I like to make this with lavender and lemons instead of limes, because lemon and lavender is such a perfect match. Of course, if you use new season's lemons they don't coincide with lavender flowering, but a few dried lavender flowers in the crust, a drop of culinary lavender essence in the filling and some crystallised lavender buds for decoration will scent and flavour the pie beautifully.

Put the biscuits, roughly broken in a heavy-duty plastic bag together with the sugar and lavender, and crush until you have fine crumbs. If you prefer, you can use the food-processor. Mix the honey and melted butter into the crumbs and press the mixture into

serves 8

12 digestive biscuits/Graham crackers
1 tablespoon light muscovado sugar
½ teaspoon dried lavender flowers
1 tablespoon honey
50 g/2 oz/½ stick unsalted butter, melted
zest and juice of 3 or 4 lemons
4 large egg yolks
400 g/14 oz can condensed milk
a drop of culinary lavender essence – optional

a 20 cm/8 inch pie dish or tin, making sure that it comes up the sides of the dish. Chill for 20 minutes to firm it and then bake at 180°C/350°F/gas mark 4 until it smells like toffee. Remove from the oven and leave to cool.

While the crust is baking, whisk the egg yolks with the lemon zest. Then beat in the condensed milk and finally stir in the lemon juice, and a drop of lavender essence if using it. The mixture will thicken – the action of the lemon juice on the condensed milk – while the crust is baking and cooling. Once cool, you can fill the crust with the mixture and bake the pie for 18 to 20 minutes at 160°C/325°F/gas mark 3. The top should not colour, but remain pale.

Once removed from the oven, let the pie cool in its container on a rack. Only serve when absolutely cold and the filling has set.

Melktert

Melktert, one of the classics of the South African kitchen, translates as 'milk tart', but it is more like a custard tart. The flavours of cinnamon and rosewater hint that the dish probably came originally from the Cape Malay tradition.

Line a 20 cm/8 inch quiche dish, or deep pie plate with the pastry. Scald the milk with the cinnamon stick and then remove the cinnamon. Stir in the butter and rosewater and thicken the milk with the cornflour slaked in a little cold milk.

serves 6

250 g/8 oz puff or flaky
    pastry – see p.120
1 litre/36 fl oz milk
4 cm/1½ inches cinnamon
    stick
1 tablespoon rosewater
50 g/2 oz/½ stick unsalted
    butter
2 tablespoons cornflour
2 to 3 tablespoons caster
    sugar
4 eggs

Stir in the sugar and beat in the egg yolks. Whisk the egg whites to stiff peaks and fold this into the mixture. Pour into the pastry case and bake in a preheated oven at 180°C/350°F/ gas mark 4 for 45 minutes or so, until just set and golden brown. This is best served warm.

Lavender honey boats

These are very pretty teatime fancies, perfect on a summer afternoon in the garden.

Grease and flour 12 boat-shaped pastry cases. Roll out the pastry and line them. Bake blind for 12 to 15 minutes and leave to cool. Cream the filling ingredients until well-mixed. Pipe or spread it in the pastry cases and leave the filled boats in a cool place to firm up. Coat the top with lavender water ice and decorate with a few flaked almonds.

makes 12

175g/6 oz short crust pastry
– see p.119

Filling

75 g/3 oz/¾ stick unsalted
butter, softened
50 g/2 oz/¼ cup caster
sugar
1 tablespoon lavender sugar
– see p.20
75 g/3 oz/½ cup ground
almonds
1 tablespoon lavender honey
a drop of culinary lavender
essence

Topping

lavender water icing
flaked almonds, lightly toasted

Saffron, mascarpone and honey tart

This recipe is based on the medieval *tarte de Bry*, versions of which I have cooked in many places; in Kuwait using *labneh* for the filling, at the British Embassy in Paris using Somerset Brie, when I cooked a gala dinner using British produce and historical recipes. Readily available mascarpone and ricotta make the perfect filling for this pale golden tart.

Soak the saffron in boiling water for 20 minutes. Roll out the pastry and line a 25 cm/10 inch rimmed pie plate. Use the trimmings to decorate the rim with pastry leaves or a plait, if liked. Bake blind for 15 to 20 minutes.

Put the mascarpone and ricotta in a bowl and mix until smooth. Dissolve the honey with the milk. Mix the honey and saffron liquid with the cheese, and beat in the eggs. Pour the mixture carefully into the pie dish and bake in a preheated oven at 190°C/375°F/gas mark 5 for 15 minutes, then turn it down to 160°C/325°F/gas mark 3 for a further 20 minutes or so. Serve warm or cold, dusted with a little icing sugar, and with or without clotted cream.

Cook's tip

Lightly toasted flaked almonds can also be used for decoration, as can a little gold leaf for a special occasion.

serves 4 to 6

$1/20$ g / 25 saffron threads soaked in 1 tablespoon boiling water

225 g/8 oz sweet or plain short crust pastry – see pp.119 and 120

225 g/8 oz/1 ½ cups mascarpone

225 g/8 oz/1 ½ cups ricotta

3 tablespoons honey

4–5 tablespoons milk

3 eggs

Caramelised mango and jasmine upside-down tart with jasmine custard

This rich tart of tropical flavours is made in the same way as a classic *tarte Tatin*, with the pastry baked on top of the caramelised fruit, and then the whole thing carefully turned over.

Generously butter a 18 or 20 cm/7 or 8 inch cake tin, then make the custard and leave it to cool and chill until required.

Bring the milk to the boil in a heavy, medium-sized saucepan and beat in the sugar, cornflour and eggs. Put the saucepan back on medium heat while stirring constantly with a wire whisk until the custard starts to thicken. Remove from the heat, whisk once more and allow to cool. Whip the cream and carefully fold it into the custard with a palette knife. Cover and keep in the fridge until ready to use.

Peel the mangoes and cut them into neat slices, lengthways. Gently melt the butter in a frying pan and dissolve the sugar in it. Raise the heat and allow the mixture to caramelise lightly. Stir in the jasmine jelly, then add the mango slices and carefully stir them in the syrupy glaze so that they are well coated.

Roll the pastry out to a round just a little bigger than the cake tin. Carefully spoon the fruit into the prepared tin, arranging neatly so that it will look attractive when turned over. Place the pastry on top of the fruit and tuck it down the side of the tin.

Bake in a preheated oven at 180°C/350°F/gas mark 4 for 25 minutes or so, until the pastry is crisp and golden. Remove from the oven and

serves 6 to 8

Custard

225 ml/8 fl oz/⅞ cup milk
1 egg plus 2 yolks, *lightly beaten with*
3 tablespoons jasmine jelly – see p.22
50g/2 oz/¼ cup sugar
25g/1 oz/3 tablespoons cornflour
50 ml/2 fl oz/¼ cup double cream

Tart

2 ripe but still firm mangoes
50 g/2 oz/½ stick unsalted butter
50 g/2 oz/¼ cup light muscovado suugar
3 tablespoons jasmine jelly – see p.22
200 g/7 oz short crust pastry
crystallised jasmine flowers – see p.19

allow to sit for a few minutes. Invert a serving plate over the tin and carefully turn out the tart, spooning any extra syrup over the fruit. Serve hot or warm, with the chilled jasmine custard.

Peach, lavender and almond tart with lavender fudge sauce

Full of the flavours and scent of summer, this is a versatile recipe and can be adapted to other fruit and flower combinations, such as gooseberry and elderflower, raspberries and roses, apricots and lavender. The floral fudge sauce is very good indeed with vanilla ice cream.

Rub the flour and butter together until well combined and crumbly, but do not overwork. Stir in the salt and sugar, and then the egg and enough iced water to bind. Wrap and cool in the refrigerator for 20 minutes before using.

Put the sugar and water in a heavy saucepan and simmer until the sugar has dissolved, then boil until the syrup turns light brown as the sugar caramelises. Stir in the cream and cook until the mixture coats the back of the spoon. Remove from the heat and add the lavender essence.

Line a 25 cm/10 inch loose-bottomed tart ring with the pastry. Flatten the almond paste, or roll it out, and line the bottom of the pastry case with it.

Slice the peaches, and arrange them over the almond. Sprinkle with lavender sugar and bake for about 45 minutes in a preheated oven at 180°C/350°F/gas mark 4. Serve warm, with the sauce.

serves 6 to 8

Pastry

225 g/8 oz/2 cups plain flour
115 g/4 oz/1 stick unsalted butter, chilled and diced
¼ teaspoon salt
50 g/2 oz/¼ cup caster sugar
1 small egg, lightly beaten
iced water – see recipe

Lavender fudge sauce

200 g/7 oz/1 scant cup granulated sugar
2 tablespoons water
300 ml/10 fl oz/1¼ cups double cream
a dash of culinary lavender essence – see p.14

To assemble and bake the tart

200 g/7 oz/1¼ cups almond paste – see p.148
6 to 8 peaches
2 tablespoons lavender sugar – see p.20
lavender fudge sauce – as above

Fig, rose and raspberry tart

Grease and flour a 25 cm/10 inch diameter tart tin or quiche dish and place it on a baking sheet.

Rub the flour and butter together until well combined and crumbly, but do not overwork. Stir in the salt and sugar, and then the egg and enough iced water to bind. Wrap and cool in the refrigerator for 20 minutes before using.

Roll out the pastry, line the tin and prick the base of the pastry all over with a fork. Cover with foil and dried beans or macaroni kept for the purpose of blind baking. Put in the top half of a preheated oven at 180°C/350°F/gas mark 4 and bake for 20 minutes. Remove the foil and 'weights'. Brush the pastry with lightly whisked egg white and return it to the oven for 5 minutes more until set. Remove from the oven and cool.

Heat the rose petal jelly in a small saucepan just until liquid. Remove from the heat and, if using it, stir in the raspberry spirit.

Arrange the fruit in the tart. Brush with half the jelly, and bake in the oven, preheated to 180°C/350°F/gas mark 4, for 10 minutes. Remove from the oven. When cool, brush with the remaining jelly and serve. Make sure that you crowd the fruit into the tart, as it will shrink on cooking and leave gaps for the pastry to show through.

serves 6 to 8

Pastry

225 g/8 oz/2 cups plain flour
115 g/4 oz/1 stick unsalted
    butter, chilled and diced
¼ teaspoon salt
50 g/2 oz/¼ cup rose petal
    sugar – see p.20
1 small egg, lightly beaten
iced water – see recipe

To assemble and bake the tart

1 tablespoon egg white,
    lightly whisked
3 or 4 tablespoons rose petal
    jelly – see p.22
eau de vie de framboise
    – optional
8 fresh, ripe unblemished figs,
    quartered
about 400 g/14 oz/2 to 3
    cups raspberries

Strawberry, rose petal and white chocolate tart in almond pastry

This is a lovely dessert for a summer Ruby Wedding celebration; in fact, you might consider, for a really special summer celebration, offering a dessert buffet based entirely around roses and strawberries and raspberries, including the previous recipe. Fruit fools, sorbets, ice-creams, jellies can all be made with these soft summer fruits, not forgetting Eton Mess, of course.

Grease and flour a 25 cm/10 inch loose-bottomed flan tin or ring set on a baking sheet.

Sift the flour and ground almonds. Rub in the butter until crumbly, stir in the sugar and add the rose essence, egg and enough water to bind to a smooth dough. Cover and chill for half an hour or so. Roll out the pastry and line the tin. The ground almonds make this quite a fragile pastry, and if you find it difficult to roll it out, press it over the base and up the side of the prepared tin; it does not matter if the edges are not even; in fact the tart looks more attractive if they are not. Prick the base all over with a fork. Line with foil or greaseproof and cover the base with ceramic baking 'beans' or dried beans.

Bake 'blind' (empty) in a preheated oven at 180°C/350°F/gas mark 4 for 20 minutes – see p.121. Remove the beans and lining paper and return the pastry to the oven for 5 to 8 minutes more to complete cooking, pricking it again if it has puffed up. Remove from the ring and cool on a wire rack.

serves 8

225 g/8 oz/2 cups plain flour

115 g/4 oz/⅔ cup ground almonds

175 g/6 oz/1 ½ sticks unsalted butter, chilled and diced

50 g/2 oz/scant ½ cup icing sugar, sifted

1 teaspoon culinary rose essence – see pp.14 and 15

1 egg, lightly beaten

iced water, as necessary

200 g/7 oz white chocolate

1 kg/2 lb/1 quart strawberries

5 tablespoons rose petal jelly – see p.22

600 ml/20 fl oz/2 ½ cups whipping cream – optional

Melt the white chocolate gently in a bowl set over hot water and brush all over the inside of the cold pastry case. Once it has set, you can fill the tart. If you wish you can, once hulled, crush most of the strawberries with the whipped cream and pile into the tart, decorating the top with the best whole strawberries, in which case you will not need the rose petal jelly.

Alternatively, pack the strawberries in the pastry, pointing skywards. Melt the rose petal jelly, allow to cool slightly but not set. Brush it over the strawberries. Serve the whipped cream separately, or, if you prefer, pouring cream, crème fraîche, vanilla ice cream or Greek yoghurt.

Lavender and lemon syllabub in an almond pastry tart

Grease and flour a tart tin measuring about 20 to 25 cm/8 to 10 inches.

Rub the flour and butter together, then use a knife to stir in the ground almonds and then the egg yolk (the white is kept for the filling), a tablespoon or so of sifted icing sugar and enough chilled water to bind it to a dough.

Wrap and chill the pastry for half an hour. Roll out the pastry and line the prepared tin. Prick all over and bake blind for 20 to 25 minutes in a preheated oven at 180°C/350°/ gas mark 4. Remove from the oven and cool.

Fresh lavender should be used for this summery recipe. You can also use elderflowers in the same way, in which case use about 8 heads of flowers, stripped from the large stalks.

serves 6

This recipe uses uncooked egg white

200 g/7 oz/1 ¾ cups plain flour

100 g/3½ oz/1 stick unsalted butter, chilled and diced

50 g/2 oz/⅓ cup ground almonds

1 egg, separated

icing sugar

chilled water

Infuse the lemon zest and lavender flowers overnight in the wine, by first heating the wine and then stirring in the lemon zest and juice and the lavender flowers.

Next day, whisk the creams to firm peaks, add the strained wine and whisk until well incorporated. In a clean bowl whisk the egg white and fold into the scented cream.

Dust the pastry case with icing sugar and spoon in the syllabub. Decorate with fresh or crystallised lavender buds.

Filling

grated zest of 1 lemon
1 teaspoon lavender flowers
4 tablespoons dessert wine
2 teaspoons lemon juice
300 ml/10 fl oz/1¼ cups
    whipping cream
300 ml/10 fl oz/1¼ cups
    double cream

Curd tart with fragrant tea-soaked sultanas

I have adapted a traditional Yorkshire recipe to include the flavour of roses in a summery, yet substantial dessert. It bears a strong resemblance to the 'dish of Curds' recipe in Robert May's *The Accomplish't Cook*, but is based on the tart my mother used to bake for special occasions.

Cover the sultanas with hot tea and let them soak. Line a greased and floured tart tin or quiche dish with the pastry. Prick the bottom and bake blind (see p.121) for 10 to 12 minutes at 200°C/400°F/gas mark 6. Let the pastry cool and lower the oven temperature to 180°C/350°F/gas mark 4. Beat the curds with the rest of the ingredients until smooth. Drain the sultanas and scatter in the bottom of the pastry case. Pour the curd mixture over them and bake for about 40 minutes until set. The surface should not brown but remain pale. Dust lightly with freshly grated nutmeg before serving.

serves 6 to 8

300 ml/10 fl oz/1¼ cups
    freshly brewed rose
    congou tea
115 g/4 oz/1 cup sultanas
225 g/8 oz sweet short crust
    pastry – see p.120
350 g/12 oz/2 cups curd
    cheese
150 ml/5 fl oz/⅝ cup single
    cream
75 g/3 oz/⅓ cup rose petal
    sugar – see p.20
1 or 2 tablespoons rosewater
grated zest of 1 lemon
freshly grated nutmeg
4 large eggs

Jasmine tea cream tart with toasted almonds

Line a greased and floured tart tin or quiche dish with the pastry. Prick the bottom and bake blind for 10 to 12 minutes at 200°C/400°F/gas mark 6. Let the pastry cool, and lower the oven temperature to 180°C/350°F/gas mark 4.

Put the milk, tea leaves and flowers in a saucepan and bring to the boil. Remove from the heat and allow to infuse for 5 minutes. Put the eggs, sugar and cream in a bowl and beat thoroughly. Strain the milk over the beaten egg mixture, and mix thoroughly. Strain into the pastry case and bake for 50 minutes or so until the tea cream has set. A knife inserted into the centre should come out clean.

Remove from the oven, cool on a wire rack and decorate before serving. This is best served just slightly warm, or at room temperature.

serves 6

225 g/8 oz sweet short crust pastry – see p.120

400 ml/14 fl oz/2 cups full cream milk

1 level tablespoon jasmine tea leaves

1 tablespoon jasmine flowers (dried will do)

2 eggs and 3 egg yolks

115 g/4 oz/½ cup caster sugar

150 ml/5 fl oz/⅝ cup double cream

For decoration

crystallised jasmine flowers, candied angelica and toasted flaked or halved almonds

Fig and rose petal jam tarts

This recipe raises the humble jam tart to new heights, especially with its scented pastry. In an ideal world, home-made fig and rose petal jam would be used. When I make it, I follow a standard strawberry jam recipe, as figs have little pectin and the same type of recipe works well. For the rose flavouring, you can add dried or fresh rose petals and boost it with a drop or two of rose essence.

Grease twelve 8 cm/3 inch tart tins, or eighteen smaller ones.

Rub the flour and butter together until well combined and crumbly, but do not overwork. Stir in the salt and sugar, and then the egg and enough iced water to bind. Wrap and cool in the refrigerator for 20 minutes before using.

Roll out the pastry and line the tart tins. Spoon in the fig jam scented with rose essence. Bake the tarts for about 15 minutes in a preheated oven at 200°C/400°F/gas mark 6. Cool on a wire rack before serving.

Cook's tip

Rose-scented strawberry jam tarts can be made in the same way, using strawberry jam. Try blackcurrant jam tarts with lavender essence and – even better – blueberry jam tarts with a hint of violet liqueur (see p.15).

makes 12 or 18

225 g/8 oz/1 cup plain flour
115 g/4 oz/1 stick unsalted
    butter, chilled and diced
a pinch of salt
1 tablespoon caster sugar
1 tablespoon rose petal sugar
    – see p.20
1 small egg, *lightly beaten with*
1 teaspoon rosewater
iced water – see recipe
fig jam – see recipe
a few drops of culinary rose
    essence – see pp.14
    and 15

Walnut and orange flower tart

This is a perfect winter recipe, for the short season for Seville oranges coincides with all the walnuts left over from holiday baking.

Grease and flour a 25 cm/10 inch pie dish. Roll out the pastry, and line the dish.

Mix the sugar and flour, and then beat in the eggs and melted butter. Stir in the nuts, and pour the mixture into the pie dish.

Bake in a preheated oven at 190°C/275°F/gas mark 5 for about 45 minutes. Serve at room temperature.

serves 8

225 g/8 oz plain short crust
    pastry – see p.119
225 g/8 oz/1 cup light
    muscovado sugar
1 tablespoon plain flour
3 eggs, *beaten with*
3 tablespoons orange flower
    water
115 g/4 oz/1 stick unsalted
    butter, melted
juice of 1 Seville orange
300 g/10 oz/3 cups walnut
    halves or pieces

Baking for special occasions

High days and holy days are when baking comes into its own, when family favourites are baked alongside traditional cakes and pastries. Easter and the Lenten period, for example, offers *colomba pasquale* in Italy, *figolli* in Malta, hot-cross buns and simnel cake in Britain, *gâteau de Paques* in Corsica, *pashka* in Russia. Many of the cakes represent religious symbols, for pastry and confectionery have often been associated with religion. Convents in Spain, Portugal and Mexico, for example, are famous for their sweets and pastries, the *dulces conventuales*, or *doces de ovos*. While each has its own speciality, many of them are based on egg yolks, especially those from convents in wine-producing areas, such as Jerez in southern Spain and Porto in Portugal. The winemakers would use the egg whites to fine their wine and then donate the yolks to the convent, a happy arrangement for both parties.

Here you will find pastries for Epiphany, for Lent and Easter, traditional cakes for Christmas from many parts of the world, as well as cakes suitable for weddings, birthdays and other family celebrations.

"They represent various symbolic figures, and now, with so many shaped pastry cutters available, the choice is wide – lambs, butterflies, rabbits, eggs, figures."

Figolli, p.146

Kwarezimal

A traditional Maltese pastry, these biscuits are, as the name suggests, made during Lent, using no eggs and no butter. Orange flower water is a traditional ingredient in many Maltese cakes and pastries, for in the eighteenth century Maltese oranges and orange flower water were famed throughout Europe, and were often sent as gifts from the Knights of Malta.

Line or grease and flour a baking sheet and preheat your oven to 190°C/375°F/gas mark 5.

Lightly toast the almonds and grind them coarsely. Mix with the ground almonds, the flour, sugar, spices and zest from the citrus fruit. Mix in the honey, the orange flower water and enough water to make a firm dough. In fact, you may need no or very little water, as the honey should provide enough moisture. Knead on a lightly floured worktop until the dough is smooth, then divide into equal size pieces. Roll into sausage shapes and place them on the prepared baking sheet. Press down lightly with your fingers along the length of the biscuits so that they take on a more oval shape.

Bake for about 20 minutes. Leave for 5 minutes or so and then transfer to a wire rack to cool. But while still hot, brush with honey and cover with toasted chopped hazelnuts or almonds.

makes 2 to 3 dozen, depending on size

225 g/8 oz/1½ cups blanched almonds
115 g/4 oz/⅔ cup ground almonds
115 g/4 oz/1 cup plain flour, sifted
150 g/5 oz/⅔ cup caster sugar
½ teaspoon ground cinnamon
½ teaspoon ground cloves
grated zest of 1 orange, 1 lemon and 1 tangerine
4 tablespoons honey
1 tablespoon orange flower water
water – see recipe

To decorate

honey – see recipe
chopped roasted hazelnuts or almonds

Figolli

Based on another traditional Maltese recipe, the best of which I have always found in the Caruana sisters' excellent book, *The Food and Cookery of Malta*, these rich almond pastries are to be found in all the islands' cake shops, especially at Easter time, but you might be lucky enough to be offered home-made *figolli*. Their main feature is that they represent various symbolic figures, and now, with so many shaped pastry cutters available, the choice is wide – lambs, butterflies, rabbits, eggs, figures. As well as the shape, the addition of a miniature Easter egg is traditional. This might be a foil-covered egg or one of the pretty speckled sugar-coated chocolate eggs.

I have reduced the recipe in the expectation that small pastry cutters will be used. Traditionally, *figolli* are very large, hand-sized pastries; smaller versions are equally attractive, and perhaps more practical.

Line or grease and flour baking sheets. The number will depend on the size of the figures you cut out. Preheat the oven to 200°C/400°F/gas mark 6.

For the pastry mix the sugar and flour, then rub in the butter until it resembles fine crumbs. Stir in the lemon zest and the egg yolk to make a pliable dough. Cover and refrigerate it while you make the almond paste.

Mix the sugar and ground almonds, then add the orange flower water, lemon zest and enough egg white to bind the mixture.

Roll out the pastry and cut out pairs of shapes,

makes 2 to 3 dozen, depending on size

Pastry

115 g/4 oz/½ cup caster sugar
225 g/8 oz/2 cups plain flour, sifted
115 g/4 oz/1 stick butter
grated zest of 1 lemon
1 egg yolk, *lightly beaten with*
1 or 2 teaspoons orange flower water

Almond paste

150 g/6 oz/1 scant cup caster or icing sugar
175 g/6 oz/1¼ cups ground almonds
1–2 teaspoons orange flower water
grated zest of 1 lemon
1 egg white

To decorate

water icing – p.24
royal icing – p.150
miniature Easter eggs

which will be sandwiched with almond paste. Lay one half of each pair on the baking sheet. Spread with almond paste, leaving a small margin. Brush this lightly with water and place the second shape on top, pressing the two lightly together.

Bake for 5 minutes and then lower the heat to 180°/350°F/gas mark 4 for 20 minutes until pale gold. Remove from the oven, place the tray on a wire rack and leave the biscuits to cool.

To decorate, coat with water icing and then pipe a design on top with royal icing in another colour. Or simply use some of the many coloured icing 'pens' and tubes available. Before the water icing has set, suitably place a miniature Easter egg.

Golden celebration sponge with gold fruit

For a fiftieth birthday, a Golden Wedding or other special occasion, this fatless sponge makes an elegant centrepiece, garnished with a rich array of exotic golden fruit. It is a perfect recipe for winter, when berry fruits are not available.

Preheat the oven to 180°C/350°F/gas mark 4. Line or grease and flour a round or square cake tin, about 20 cm/8 inches in diameter or equivalent.

Put half the sugar in a pudding basin and set over a saucepan of hot water. Add the egg yolks and whisk until thick and pale. This will take about 5 minutes, during which time you should also whisk in the orange zest, saffron threads and soaking liquid. Whisk the egg

serves 4 to 6

$^1/_{20}$ g/25 saffron threads soaked in 1 tablespoon boiling water

115 g/4 oz/½ cup caster sugar

4 eggs, separated

grated zest of 1 orange

115 g/4 oz/1 cup self-raising flour, sifted

whites together with half the remaining sugar until peaks form. Fold in the rest of the sugar and whisk until firm and glossy. Fold the sifted flour into the egg yolk mixture and then fold in the egg white mixture. Spoon into the tin, shaking to fill it evenly. Bake for 10 to 12 minutes, until just firm to the touch. Turn out onto a cake rack to cool.

Halve the cake. Whip the cream and fold in the saffron threads and liquid and also the passion fruit pulp. Spread one half of the cake with the cream. Whichever fruit you choose should be sliced or halved as appropriate, piled on the cream and the top half of the cake replaced. Dust with icing sugar before serving. When using kumquats in the cake, I often halve them and poach them gently with extra passion fruit pulp and sugar.

Filling

300 ml/10 fl oz/1⅓ cups double cream

1/20 g/25 saffron threads soaked in 1 tablespoon boiling milk

2 or 3 passion fruit, halved and the pulp sieved

Some or all of the following, peeled, sliced or otherwise prepared as appropriate: physallis sharon fruit kumquats mango

icing sugar for sifting

Golden celebration cake

As an alternative for a fiftieth birthday or Golden Wedding, a christening or other family party, this is the perfect cake because, like a traditional Christmas cake, it can be baked well in advance of the event, and will only get better with keeping. This is usually my recipe of choice for Christmas too.

Line a deep cake tin, 22 cm/9 inches in diameter, with several layers of baking parchment or greaseproof on the base and sides.

Cream the butter and sugar and then add the flour and eggs alternately. Beat in the orange flavourings. Set a sieve over the mixing bowl and strain any liquid from the soaked fruit

serves 8 to 10

225 g/8 oz/2 sticks unsalted butter

200 g/7 oz/1 scant cup light muscovado sugar

4 eggs

300 g/10 oz/1½ cups plain flour, sifted

75 ml/3 fl oz/⅓ cup orange juice

2–3 tablespoons orange flower water

2 tablespoons finely grated orange zest

into the cake batter. Move the sieve away and toss the fruit in a couple of tablespoons or so of flour to 'mop up' any excess liquid from the fruit, otherwise it may sink to the bottom of the cake. Stir in the fruit, the almonds and spices. Spoon the mixture into the prepared cake tin. Make a slight hollow in the middle and bake for 2½ to 3 hours at 150°C/300°F/ gas mark 2, or until a skewer inserted in the middle comes out clean. When cool, wrap well and store until you want to decorate it. A cake this size takes about 450 g/1 lb marzipan or almond paste, as below.

1.25 kg/2½ lb dried fruit, the more golden the better, such as apricots, sultanas, peaches, mango and mixed citrus peel, all soaked overnight in 150 ml/5 fl oz/¾ cup almond or orange liqueur
115 g/4 oz/¾ cup flaked almonds
1 teaspoon powdered mace
1 teaspoon ground cardamom
1 tablespoon mixed spice

Almond paste

Almond paste or marzipan is ideal for large fruit cakes such as Christmas and wedding cakes that will be stored for some time. The thick covering helps keep the cake moist, as well as adding an extra layer of richness. Home-made marzipan is very easy to make, simply by mixing together the ground almonds, sugars and orange flower water with enough egg to make a firm, pliable paste. Roll out as required, using a little sifted icing sugar on the worktop to prevent sticking.

225 g/8 oz/1 ⅓ cups ground almonds
175 g/6 oz/1 cup icing sugar
175 g/6 oz/¾ cup caster sugar
1–2 teaspoons orange flower water
whites of 2 small eggs for white marzipan *or*
yolks of 2 small eggs for yellow marzipan

Cook's tip

If you are making almond paste for a rose-scented cake, use rosewater in place of the orange flower water.

Royal icing

This is suitable for Christmas cakes and other celebration cakes and gives a highly professional finish. It is best used on top of marzipan, and the cake iced two or three days in advance to allow it to set.

Sift the icing sugar into a large bowl. Stir in the lemon juice, the egg whites, any colouring and floral essence. When fully mixed, the icing will stand in peaks when stirred and lifted with a palette knife. Ice the cake as required. A very simple method is to spread it all over the cake with a broad palette knife, then form it into small peaks or points with the tip of the knife. Otherwise, work quickly dipping the knife in hot water from time to time (and shaking off excess water) and aim for broad, smooth strokes for a flat surface. Leave it to harden before decorating further. Any remaining icing can be covered with cling film and used to add flowers or letters to the surface once the main icing has hardened.

450 g/1 lb/3 ⅓ cups icing sugar
whites of 2 eggs
2 teaspoons lemon juice, sieved
colouring
orange flower water or floral essence

Floral *panforte*

I have adapted this from a traditional holiday speciality full of spices, dried fruit and nuts, from Siena and Perugia in central Italy. Dried flowers replace most of the spices – you can choose which flavouring you prefer. You can also adapt the recipe to orange flavours, using candied orange peel alone or orange marmalade, as well as orange flower water.

Line a 20 cm/8 inch round sponge tin with rice paper or greased baking parchment and

serves 8 to 10

175 g/6 oz/1 ½ cups plain flour
1 tablespoon ground mixed spice
1 teaspoon ground cardamom
1 teaspoon dried lavender flowers *or* several drops culinary lavender essence *or*

preheat the oven to 180°C/350°F/gas mark 4.

Thoroughly combine the flour, cardamom and flowers in a large bowl, and add the fruit, nuts and candied citrus peel. Gently heat the honey in a saucepan for 2 minutes then pour it over the mixture in the bowl, stirring thoroughly to blend the sticky mass. Spoon it into the prepared tin and, with oiled fingers, pack the mixture down well. Dust the top with a mixture of cornflour, icing sugar and a little cinnamon and bake in the centre of the oven for about 35 minutes. Lift onto a wire rack and do not cut until the panforte is completely cold.

1 tablespoon dried rose petals *and* a few drops of rose essence

300 g/10 oz/⅞ cup clear honey

225 g/8 oz/2 cups whole blanched almonds, lightly toasted and chopped

175 g/6 oz/1½ cups un-dyed mixed candied citrus peel

75 g/3 oz/⅓ cup un-dyed glacé cherries

Chestnut tartlets

This is based on a traditional Maltese recipe, *pastizzotti tal-qastan*, which I first came across in *The Food and Cookery of Malta* by Anne and Helen Caruana Galizia. Chestnuts are much used in winter cooking in the Maltese islands and *imbuljuta*, a thick and warming chestnut, orange and chocolate 'soup', is served after Christmas midnight mass. I have used the orange flavouring in these crisp pies, perfect for an afternoon tea over the Christmas holidays, instead of mince pies.

Peel the chestnuts; simmer until they are soft. Grind them in a food-processor or pass through a food mill. Moisten, if necessary, with a little water, but the final purée should be dry. Add the other filling ingredients. Taste and adjust for sweetness. Leave to cool.

Roll the pastry, line 12 greased tartlet tins with it and fill with the chestnut mixture. Either lay a cross of two pastry strips, or cover

makes 12

600 g/20 oz fresh chestnuts

1 tablespoon good orange marmalade

50 g/2 oz bitter chocolate, melted

grated rind of 1 lemon and 1 tangerine

1 teaspoon caster sugar

2–3 teaspoons orange flower water

plain or sweet short crust pastry made with 300 g/ 10 oz/2¾ cups flour – see pp.119 or 120

1 tablespoon beaten egg for glazing

each tartlet with a pastry lid, in which you cut a cross with scissors through which the filling will show. Glaze with beaten egg. Bake at 200°C/400°F/gas 6 for 15 to 20 minutes. Cool on a wire rack.

Cook's tip

You can also used dried chestnuts, canned chestnuts, whole vacuum packed chestnuts or unsweetened chestnut purée. Sweetened chestnut purée is available, but if you use it, omit the sugar and marmalade and add extra tangerine zest.

Orange flower marzipan and mincemeat tart

For a bake-ahead dessert to serve after the Christmas turkey, or for a Boxing Day buffet, I have developed this recipe for a large mince tart with rich orange flower and marzipan flavours. Less fiddly than individual mince pies, this makes a very attractive tray bake. Make it in a Swiss roll tin and top with a lattice of pastry if you wish. The layer of marzipan under the mincemeat makes this an even richer than usual mince tart.

Dress up commercial mincemeat by pouring a generous splash of Grand Marnier or Cointreau and a spoonful or two of orange flower water into the jar before you start making the pastry, and preferably two or three days before you plan to use it.

Rub the flour and butter together, by hand or in a food-processor. Stir in the sugar, zest, juice and enough orange flower water to bind, adding iced water if necessary. Line a standard Swiss roll tin with greased baking parchment.

serves 10 to 12

400 g/14 oz/3½ cups plain flour

200 g/7 oz/1¾ sticks unsalted butter, chilled and diced

2 tablespoons caster sugar

grated zest of 2 oranges

juice of 1 orange, chilled

1–2 tablespoons orange flower water

225 g/8 oz almond paste – see p.149

400 g/14 oz jar mincemeat – see below

Cut the paper long enough for you to use it to
ease the baked tart out of the tin. Divide the
pastry in half. Roll out one piece to fit the tin.
Roll out the marzipan as thinly as possible to
fit on top of the pastry, cutting and patching if
necessary, but leave a plain border of about
½ cm/⅛ inch to allow the mixture to spread.
Brush the border with milk.

Spoon the mincemeat on top and spread it
to the border. Roll out the second piece of
pastry to fit and press it down to seal the
edges. Decorate the edges with a fork or spoon
handle if you wish. Prick the pastry all over
with a fork and bake at 180°C/350°F/gas mark
4 for about 35 minutes, until the pastry is crisp
and pale golden. Remove from the oven and
carefully transfer from the tin to a wire rack
after about 5 to 10 minutes cooling in the tin.

Cut into squares or fingers for serving, dusted
with icing sugar. Serve warm as a pudding
with orange flower custard or mandarin ice
cream. When cold, cut in smaller pieces for
teatime pastries.

Stollen 1

There are those who admit to no variations
on a traditional recipe. Some years ago in one
of my newspaper columns, I gave a recipe for
Stollen, the German tea bread, and suggested
that, as a yeast bread, it was also rather good to
eat at breakfast, as one might a Danish pastry.
A reader wrote to me with her recipe, which
she had used for years and, she claimed, was
totally authentic, made with pastry rather than
yeast, and was certainly not a breakfast bread.
In the same post I received a letter from my

friend Claire Clark, world-renowned pastry chef, with her *Stollen* recipe. Like mine, it was a yeast-based recipe. Both versions are very good. The non-yeast version improves with keeping and I have adapted the recipes further to include the merest hint of rose.

Sprinkle the yeast on the milk and leave until it froths. Sift flour and salt into a bowl and rub in the butter. Add the mandarin zest and juice, fruit, nuts, then the yeast mixture and egg. Mix to a dough and knead for 10 minutes. Cover and leave to rise until doubled in bulk. Knock back and knead the dough for a few minutes, then roll into a long oval. Roll the marzipan into a cylinder and place down the length of the dough slightly to one side. Fold over the dough and pinch down to seal. Place on a greased baking sheet, sealed side down.

Cover with a clean damp cloth and leave to rise in warm place for 40 minutes or until doubled in size. Bake in preheated oven at 200°C/400°F/gas mark 6 for 35 to 45 minutes until well risen and golden brown. Transfer to a wire rack to cool. Dust with icing sugar before serving. The top can be glazed before baking if you like. An alternative presentation is to dip the loaf in melted butter while still hot, and then dredge with caster sugar.

makes 10 to 12 slices

2 teaspoons dried yeast

up to 200 ml/7 oz/¾ cup warm milk plus pinch of sugar

450 g/1 lb/4 cups strong plain flour

½ teaspoon salt

150 g/5 oz/1 ¼ sticks unsalted butter

grated zest and juice of 1 mandarin

225 g/8 oz/2 cups mixed, dried fruit chopped to even size

75 g/3 oz/¾ cup chopped almonds

1 egg, *beaten with*

2 tablespoons orange flower water

225 g/8 oz almond paste – p.149

Stollen 2

Put the flour in a bowl. Make a hollow and in it put the sugar, seasoning, spices and eggs, then mix thoroughly. Add the remaining ingredients. Knead thoroughly, shape into a loaf and place on a greased baking tray. Bake in a preheated oven at 160°C/325°F/gas mark 3 for about 75 minutes. While still hot, brush with the melted butter and dredge with icing sugar. Allow to cool completely before storing in a tin.

makes 10 to 12 slices

450 g/1 lb/4 cups self-raising flour
200 g/7 oz/1 scant cup caster sugar
a pinch of salt
a few drops of culinary rose essence
4 tablespoons rum, *Kirschwasser* or *eau de vie de framboise*
zest of 1 lemon
1 teaspoon *each* ground cardamom and nutmeg
2 eggs, *beaten with*
2 tablespoons rose water
200 g/7 oz/1 ¾ sticks unsalted butter, diced
225 g/8 oz/1 ⅔ cup cream cheese
115 g/4 oz/1 cup each of currants, raisins and chopped almonds
50 g/2 oz/½ cup candied mixed peel

To finish

50 g/2 oz/½ stick unsalted butter, melted
50 g/2 oz/scant ½ cup icing sugar

Bûche de Noël, chocolate and orange log

French *pâtisserie* windows are a delight at any time of the year, but by the middle of December they are filled with beautifully decorated *bûches de Noël*, which always inspire me. The cake part is not difficult to make; the skill and creativity lies in the decorating. One year I offered to make the dessert for a Christmas party and chose to make a large chocolate *bûche*. I made four Swiss rolls, cutting one of them into angled pieces, so that I could join the rolls other than in a straight line, and some pieces I used for 'knots'. As someone said, it looked rather more like a branch than a log when I had finished with it.

Line a Swiss roll tin with buttered greaseproof paper.

Whisk half the sugar and the egg yolks in a bowl set in a pan over – but not touching – simmering water until pale and foamy, and the mixture leaves a ribbon when trailed on the surface.

With a clean whisk, beat the egg whites with the remaining sugar until firm and glossy. Fold together the yolk mixture, flour and cocoa and egg whites, adding the orange zest, liqueur and orange flower water.

Pour the cake batter into the prepared tin. Smooth the surface and bake in a preheated oven at 180°C/350°F/gas mark 4 for 12 to 15 minutes, or until the sponge begins to shrink away from the side of the tin.

Remove from the oven, turn out onto a damp clean tea towel, peel off the paper, trim off the

serves 6

Sponge

115 g/4 oz/½ cup caster sugar

3 eggs, separated

75 g/3 oz/¾ cup plain flour, *sifted with*

1 tablespoon cocoa powder

grated zest of 1 mandarin orange

1 tablespoon orange liqueur

2 tablespoons orange flower water

Filling

115 g/4 oz chocolate, at least 70% cocoa solids

3 tablespoons double cream

a few drops each of orange flower water and orange liqueur

115 g/4 oz/1 stick unsalted butter, diced, softened but not melted

50 g/2 oz/scant ½ cup sifted icing sugar

chocolate shavings and crystallised orange zest for decoration crusty edges, then loosely and gently roll the cake while you prepare the filling.

For the filling, break up the chocolate and melt it in the cream, in a *bain-marie*, then mix in the other ingredients until you have a butter cream of thick, spreading consistency. Unroll the sponge, spread with half the filling, and re-roll it. Spread the remaining cream over the roll and mark with a fork to represent bark on a log. Decorate with the chocolate shavings and crystallised orange peel and serve the same day.

White chocolate mousse and orange flower roulade

Here is a pale and elegant partner to the chocolate log, both of them ideal as alternatives to the rich fruitcakes and puddings of the Christmas table.

Preheat the oven to 180°C/350°F/gas mark 4. Grease and line a Swiss roll tray with greaseproof paper.

Put half the sugar in a pudding basin set over a pan of hot water. Separate the eggs, putting the whites to one side in a large bowl and the yolks with the sugar in the basin. Whisk this mixture until thick and pale. This will take about 5 minutes, during which time you should also whisk in the orange flower water.

Start beating the egg whites, together with half the remaining sugar until peaks form. Fold in the rest of the sugar and whisk until firm and glossy. Grate the orange zest and mix it into the egg yolks, together with the sifted flour, and then fold in the egg white mixture.

serves 6 to 8

Sponge

115 g/4 oz/½ cup caster sugar

3 large eggs

1 tablespoon orange flower water

115 g/4 oz/1 cup self-raising flour, sifted

1 orange

Filling

100 g/3½ oz white chocolate

1 teaspoon orange flower water

150 ml/5 oz/¾ cup double cream

50 g/2 oz/½ stick unsalted butter

1 egg white

Spoon this into the Swiss roll tray, shaking and tapping it to fill it evenly. Bake for 10 to 12 minutes, until just firm to the touch. Turn out flat onto a clean tea towel. Peel off the paper and trim off the firm edges. Roll up loosely, from one of the short ends, wrapping the tea towel with it, and leave to cool while you prepare the filling.

Break the chocolate into small pieces and put in a bowl. Bring the orange flower water and half the cream to the boil and pour it over the chocolate. Stir until the chocolate has melted and allow it to cool. When almost cool, stir in the butter. Whip the remaining cream and separately whisk the egg white. Fold the two together and fold into the white chocolate mixture. Unroll the sponge, and remove the paper. Spread the filling over the sponge and reroll it. Place on a long platter, and sift icing sugar over it. Decorate with fresh or crystallised flowers and/or zest.

To finish

icing sugar
fresh edible flowers,
    crystallised flowers *or*
    crystallised orange zest

St Stephen's cake

'Deep and crisp and even', that is the simple topping for this cake, icing sugar thickly dredged on an orange-scented crystallised fruit cake. Easy to make at the last minute and, with the ingredients almost certainly to hand, this is a very good cake for tea on Boxing Day, the feast of St Stephen.

Grease and flour a 20 cm/8 inch cake tin.

Cream the butter and sugar until light and fluffy. Beat the whole eggs and egg yolks with the orange flower water and gradually beat into the cake mixture, alternating with the

serves 8 to 10

200 g/7 oz/1¾ sticks
    unsalted butter, softened
200 g/7 oz/1 scant cup
    caster sugar
4 eggs, 2 of them separated
2 tablespoons orange flower
    water
200 g/7 oz/1¾ cups self-
    raising flour
1 tablespoon grated orange
    zest
1 tablespoon orange juice

flour, which you fold in. Stir in the remaining ingredients, then whisk the egg whites and fold those in.

Spoon into the prepared cake tin, smooth the top and bake in a preheated oven at 180°C/350°F/gas mark 4, for about 50 minutes. When the cake is cooked, a skewer inserted in the middle will emerge clean. Transfer the cake to a wire rack to cool, and then sift on a thick layer of icing sugar before serving. If you wish, you can cut the cake in half and fill with an orange flower butter cream and spread an orange flower water icing on top.

75 g/3 oz/¾ cup chopped glacé or crystallised orange, kumquat or mandarin
25 g/1 oz/2 tablespoons flaked or chopped blanched almonds
icing sugar

A frosted log

Inspired by a New Year's Eve spent in Paris, this is a variation on my white chocolate mousse and orange flower roulade first published in my *Times Cookbook* and makes a perfect *bûche* for *le Réveillon*. It would also make a pretty centrepiece for a christening tea for a baby girl. You can adapt the recipe to violet and lavender flavours.

Preheat your oven to 180°C/350°F/gas mark 4. Grease a Swiss roll tin, and line with greaseproof paper.

Put half the sugar in a bowl set over a saucepan of hot water. Add the egg yolks and whisk until thick and pale. This will take about five minutes, whisking by hand, much less with an electric whisk, during which time you should also whisk in the rum and rosewater.

Whisk the egg whites, together with half the remaining sugar, until peaks form. Fold in the rest of the sugar and whisk until firm and

serves 8

Cake

75 g/3 oz/⅓ cup caster sugar
25 g/1 oz/1 tablespoon rose petal sugar
4 eggs, separated
1 tablespoon white rum
1 tablespoon rosewater
2 tablespoons ground almonds
115 g/4 oz/1 cup self-raising flour, sifted

glossy. Fold the ground almonds and sifted flour into the egg yolk mixture, then fold in the egg white mixture. Spoon the cake mixture into the Swiss roll tin, shaking it to get rid of air pockets.

Bake for 10 to 12 minutes, until just firm to the touch. Turn out onto a clean tea towel. Peel off the paper and trim off the firm edges. Roll up, from one of the short ends, wrapping the tea towel with it. Leave to cool while you prepare the filling.

To prepare the filling, soak the gelatine in water to soften it and then stir in the rosewater and rum. Heat gently until the gelatine has dissolved and allow to cool. Melt the chocolate and add to the gelatine mix. Whip the cream and fold this in, then finally whisk the egg white and fold into the chocolate cream.

Allow the mousse to almost set, and then unroll the sponge, spread with mousse and re-roll. Place on a serving plate and decorate. Mix icing sugar with a drop of lemon juice and enough rosewater to make a thin, spreadable glaze and use it to cover the sponge. While it is still tacky, scatter the white chocolate shavings and rose petals on top. As a fatless sponge, this cake is best eaten the same day.

Filling

2 sheets or 2 level teaspoons gelatine
2 tablespoons white rum
1 tablespoon rosewater
100 g/3½ oz white chocolate
150 ml/6 fl oz/¾ cup double cream
1 egg white

To decorate

icing sugar
lemon juice
a few drops of rosewater or culinary rose essence – see pp.14 and 15
thin shavings of white chocolate
crystallised rose petals – see p.19

Twelfth Night cakes

Here are two recipes for the last day of the
Christmas season. In the south and south-
west of France a *fouace*, or *fougasse*, is served at
Epiphany. Hearth bread, oven-bottom cake,
foccacia, *fougasse*, *fouace*, *hogaza*, *pogacsa*, breads
from many different countries, are cooked
on the hearthstone – *focus* in Latin – or in the
bottom of the oven. The bread is shaped into
a flattish round, baked until it has risen and
then turned over to bake the top crust. Further
north, the cake is likely to be a *galette*, filled
with a perfumed almond mix.

Fouace

Mix the yeast and warm water and a little of
the sugar in a bowl. Once it begins to froth,
stir in the eggs, floral water, salt and the rest
of the sugar. Add half the flour and work it
thoroughly for 5 minutes or so, gradually
adding the butter, which should be soft and
creamy but not oily. Finally, add the remaining
flour and knead or work with a spatula until
you have an elastic mixture which sticks to
itself rather than your hands. Cover with
cling film and let the dough prove all day in
a relatively cool place, such as a north-facing
kitchen window sill.

Then knock it back, cover again and leave in
the refrigerator overnight. Turn it out onto a
floured worktop, knead again simply to expel
all the air, and then roll it out to resemble a
large oval pitta bread and not much thicker.
Nick the edges with scissors at intervals, and
transfer it to a baking sheet. Let it double in

serves 4 to 6

2 teaspoons dried yeast
3 tablespoons warm water
4 eggs, *lightly beaten with*
1 tablespoon orange flower
    water *or* rosewater
2 teaspoons salt
25 g/1 oz/1 tablespoon
    caster sugar
450 g/1 lb/4 cups plain flour,
    sifted
150 g/5 oz/1¼ sticks
    unsalted butter, softened

volume before putting it in a preheated oven at 230°C/450°F/gas mark 8 for 20 minutes. Remove from the oven, and allow it to cool on a wire rack before serving.

Candied peel can be added to the dough before baking, and the crust can be brushed with the scented water again after baking.

Galette

Mix the almonds, butter, sugar and orange flower water together. Roll out the pastry to two circles about 20 to 22 cm/8 to 9 inches in diameter. Place one circle on a baking sheet, lined with greaseproof paper, and spread the almond mixture over it, leaving a 2 cm/ ¾ inch border. Push the bean into the almond mixture and smooth over it.

Brush around the border with a little of the egg and milk glaze, then lay the second circle of pastry on top. Press down lightly with the prongs of a fork to seal. Prick the top in one or two places and decorate with pastry trimmings, or by marking it decoratively with a sharp knife. Brush with the glaze.

Bake in a preheated oven at 200°C/400°F/ gas mark 6 for 15 to 20 minutes until well-risen and golden brown. The finder of the bean becomes king or queen of the Twelfth Night festivities.

serves 6

150 g/5 oz/1 cup ground almonds

75 g/3 oz/¾ stick unsalted butter, softened

75 g/3 oz/⅓ cup caster sugar

1 tablespoon orange flower water

300 g/10 oz puff pastry – see p.121

1 china bean or dried haricot bean

½ egg yolk, *beaten with*

1 tablespoon milk *and*

2 teaspoons orange flower water, to glaze

Wedding cakes with a difference

Different countries have different traditions when it comes to wedding cakes. In Scandinavia ring cakes of ground almond and egg white of increasing size are stacked on top of each other in a *kransekake*. In France the celebratory cake is likely to be a *croquembouche*. This is a light and airy confection of small balls of choux pastry, filled with pastry cream and constructed into a tall cone, the balls stuck together with a dab of caramel, more of which is drizzled over the surface. I cannot count how many times I have seen junior pastry chefs producing these towers in cookery competitions; so often it ends in tears, as the pastry sags and the caramel melts. Nevertheless, when properly done, it has a real wow factor and makes a change from the 'marble mausoleum' of the traditional tiered wedding cake with stiff icing and heavy fruit cake balanced on pillars.

Of course, the reason for such a solid cake in the first place was that the top tier would be removed, wrapped and stored, to be served at the christening of the first born, while the second tier would be cut up and sent to distant relatives. You cannot do either of those with a prettily decorated sponge cake or a *croquembouche*, nor with a more recent fashion, which is a tiered arrangement of pastel-coloured or otherwise themed cup cakes. This makes a very attractive centrepiece for a small informal wedding party, as it does for other celebrations. And the pastel-coloured cakes can have a matching floral flavour; orange flower water, rose, violet, lavender, jasmine, saffron.

In fact, this is a fashion which has come full circle, for in medieval England it was the custom for guests to bring small cakes to the wedding, where they would be iced and stuck together to form a tower, over which the bridal couple would kiss and endeavour not to knock over the tower. Who knows what ill-luck would follow? The custom gradually changed to the cakes, known as bride cakes, being provided by the bride, but the format remained the same until well into the eighteenth century when the wedding cake became the egg-rich fruit cake of modern times.

I came across a clever idea recently, the brain-child of a young doctor and his friends who were baking a wedding cake. The bottom tier was a traditional fruit cake, then a smaller, rich chocolate cake for the middle tier and finally an airy sponge cake. I never did get round to finding out how it was to be decorated, but I like the idea. Were I to recreate a floral version, I would use the golden celebration cake from this chapter as the first layer, the lavender chocolate cake mix on p.61 for the middle tier and, for the top, a violet cassata, p.60.

A glance at the baking section of the Lakeland website www.lakeland.co.uk will provide you with plenty of inspiration for presentation of your cake or cakes, should you decide to bake your own wedding centrepiece. And one of the best shops for the cake maker that I have ever come across is to be found in Oxford's Covered Market – if cakes are your thing, it is well worth a visit. From the romantic to the classical, the avant-garde to the frankly

humorous, they produce all manner of cakes
for special occasions. But the shop, on-line at
www.the-cakeshop.co.uk also sells every item
you could possibly need for baking, sugarcraft
and cake decorating, and some you did not
even know you could not do without, from
icing in many colours, nozzles and icing bags,
boards and ribbons, a whole section devoted
to cup cakes and sturdy boxes of every size for
you to send a piece of wedding cake to your
cousins in Tasmania.

Love cake

Sri Lanka also has the custom of sharing the
wedding cake, in this case the charmingly-
named love cake. Although not a rich fruit
cake, its spices, honey and sugar preserve it
well enough to send a piece home with all
the guests. From the number of eggs required
for the traditional recipe, a dozen in some
recipes, 7 or 10 in others, it is without doubt a
remnant of the Portuguese presence in Ceylon.
The original Portuguese recipe would have
contained ground almonds, which are replaced
today by cashew nuts, one of Sri Lanka's main
crops. When I was in Colombo as guest chef, I
met some delightful cooks and cookery writers
who shared their recipes with me, and this
recipe is based on some of those. If you cannot
get the large quantity of cashew nuts, do, by all
means, use ground almonds. Like many cakes
made with honey – 'bees' honey' as specified
in all the love cake recipes I have studied – or
syrup, it improves with keeping, so should
be made a few days before required. As one
might imagine from the ingredients, this cake
also makes a delicious dessert, warm or cold,

serves 10

6 eggs, separated
400 g/14 oz/1¾ cups soft
    brown sugar
200 g/7 oz/1 cup semolina
115 g/4 oz/1 stick unsalted
    butter, softened but not
    oily
175 g/6 oz/1¼ cups ground
    almonds or ground cashew
    nuts
2 tablespoons rose water
2 tablespoons honey
½ teaspoon *each* ground
    cloves, cinnamon,
    cardamom and nutmeg
1 teaspoon grated lime or
    lemon zest
icing sugar – see recipe

especially when served with pure vanilla ice cream, or, even better, with rose petal ice cream; it would be perfect for the wedding breakfast.

Preheat the oven to 150°C/300°F/gas mark 3.

Grease and line two 20 cm/8 inch square or round cake tins, or a heart-shaped tin of similar volume.

Put the egg yolks and sugar in a bowl and beat until pale and thick. In another bowl mix the semolina and butter and add this to the egg mixture. Beat this well then fold in the ground nuts, rosewater, honey, spices and zest. Whisk the egg whites to firm peaks then fold them into the cake batter. Spoon the batter into the prepared tins, smooth the surface and bake for about 1 to 1½ hours, until the cake is golden brown on top and cooked through. Note, however, that this is a moist cake. Allow the cake to cool in the tin, cut it into squares, dust with icing sugar and arrange nicely on a platter or cake stand.

Cook's tip

If you want a crusty topping, thickly dust the cake with icing sugar *before* baking. A really pretty wedding centre-piece would be to bake one large love cake and then a batch of small ones, also heart-shaped.

Floral *gâteau St Honoré*

It would be remiss in a book of baking not to pay *hommage* to Saint Honoré, the patron saint of, amongst others, pastry cooks, so here is a version of 'his' traditional cake. Often made with praline or coffee cream, a rose-scented version makes a wonderful centrepiece for a special occasion, as it is somewhat laborious, although not difficult, to make. A pastry base, choux pastry surround, pastry cream filling and whipped cream topping, with a little caramel here and a few crystallised rose petals there, the various stages can be made in advance.

If you prefer, use commercial all-butter puff pastry for the base, or half quantities of the flaky pastry on p.120.

Line two baking sheets with silicone. Preheat the oven to 230°C/450°F/gas mark 8.

In a small, heavy-based saucepan bring the water, butter and salt to the boil and, when it does so, tip in all the flour at once, stirring vigorously with a wooden spoon. As you stir, the mixture will dry and become smooth to the point where it leaves the sides of the pan. Remove from the heat and beat in the eggs, a little at a time, making sure each addition is thoroughly incorporated. Because the absorbent quality of flour can change from batch to batch and can vary with the day's humidity, it is a good idea not to add the whole of the second egg, as you may not need it all to give you a soft, pliable but not liquid dough. On the other hand, if the flour is very dry, you may need to add a little more beaten

serves 6 to 8

Choux paste

115 ml/4 oz/½ cup water
50 g/2 oz/½ stick unsalted butter
a pinch of salt
75 g/3 oz/¾ cup plain flour
2 eggs, *lightly beaten with*
1 tablespoon rosewater

Base

115 g/4 oz/½ cup plain flour
50 g/2 oz/½ stick unsalted butter, chilled and diced
a pinch of salt
25 g/1 oz/1 tablespoon rose petal sugar – see p.20
1 small egg, lightly beaten
iced water – see recipe

Pastry cream

225 ml/8 fl oz/1 cup milk
1 egg plus 2 yolks, lightly beaten
50g/2 oz/¼ cup sugar
25g/1 oz/3 tablespoons cornflour
50 ml/2 fl oz/¼ cup double cream
4 tablespoons rosewater *or* a few drops culinary rose essence to taste – see pp.14 and 15

egg. At this point, too, add any flavourings. Keep stirring until you have a smooth paste.

Cover with damp greaseproof paper to prevent a crust from forming while you prepare the rest of the cake.

Make the pastry base by rubbing the flour and butter together until well combined and crumbly, but do not overwork. Stir in the salt and sugar, and then the egg and enough iced water to bind. Wrap and cool in the refrigerator for 20 minutes before using.

To make the pastry cream, bring the milk to the boil in a medium, heavy-based saucepan and beat in the sugar, cornflour and eggs. Put the saucepan back on a medium heat while stirring constantly with a wire whisk until the custard starts to thicken. Remove from the heat, whisk once more and allow to cool. When the custard is almost cold, stir in the rosewater or essence. Whip the cream and carefully fold it into the custard with a palette knife. Cover and keep in the fridge until ready to use.

Roll out the pastry to make a circle 25 cm/10 inches in diameter and place it on the baking sheet. Prick the pastry all over. Using three-quarters of the choux paste, pipe or spoon it around the edges of the pastry base forming a complete ring, about 5 cm/2 ½ inches wide, with a 1 cm/½ inch border of pastry showing.

Bake the base for about 25 minutes. Remove from the oven and allow to cool on a wire rack. Form 6 to 8 balls with the remaining choux paste and place these on the second baking tray. Bake for about 15 minutes at the same temperature and cool them on a wire rack.

To finish

115 g/4 oz/½ cup granulated sugar
115 ml/4 fl oz/½ cup water
300 ml/10 fl oz/1 ¼ cups whipping cream
a dash of pink colouring
1 tablespoon rosewater or a few drops of rose essence
2 dozen or so crystallised rose petals – see p.19
50 g/2 oz/½ cup flaked almonds, lightly toasted

You cannot bake the two at the same time, as the base takes longer than the buns, and the secret to well-risen choux pastry is to cook at an even temperature without opening the oven door.

While the pastry is baking, make a light caramel by dissolving the sugar in the water and boiling until it reaches 140°C/275°F, the 'crack' stage, when a drop of syrup forms brittle threads if dropped into cold water.

Dip the base of the choux buns in the caramel and stick them to the choux pastry border at intervals.

Whip the cream, adding a dash of flavouring and colouring. Fill the centre of the cake with the rose-scented pastry cream and pipe the whipped cream on top, as decoratively as you like, in swirls and peaks. Just before serving, scatter on the rose petals and flaked almonds.

Rose petal *croquembouche*

For an engagement party, a wedding, a baby shower, a christening or other special occasion when an impressive centrepiece is required, it is worth taking the time and effort to make this spectacularly pretty tower of rose-scented, rose pink choux buns. But only attempt it on a dry day in a cool kitchen when you have plenty of time.

Grease and flour or line two baking sheets with silicone or baking parchment.

Bring the milk, butter, sugar and salt to the boil in a medium-sized saucepan. Add the flour in one go and mix it vigorously until it

makes 36 pieces

For the choux buns

225 ml/8 fl oz/1 cup semi-skimmed milk

115 g/4 oz/1 stick unsalted butter

40 g/2½ oz/¼ cup caster sugar

½ coffeespoon salt

150 g/5 oz/1¼ cups plain flour

4 eggs

leaves the sides of the pan. Remove from the heat. After a few minutes, when the mixture has cooled somewhat, beat in the eggs, one at a time. Spoon the paste into an icing bag with a round 10 mm nozzle. Pipe 36 small heaps, about 2 cm/barely 1 inch in diameter, onto the prepared sheets, well spaced out. Bake for 20 to 25 minutes at 190°C/375°F/gas mark 5, until light golden brown. Transfer to a wire rack to cool.

Beat the egg yolks in a bowl with the sugar and syrup, then blend in the flour. Bring the milk to the boil and pour it onto the egg and flour mixture, whisking continuously. Transfer to a saucepan and let it thicken over a low heat, stirring all the while for about 5 minutes. Once slightly cooled, cover the custard with cling film and then refrigerate for a couple of hours. I do not recommend colouring the custard; the egg yolks make it quite yellow and it risks taking on an orange tint if you add red or pink colouring.

Spoon the custard into a piping bag with a 10 mm nozzle. Make a small hole in the base of each choux bun and fill with the rose-scented custard.

Make a soft icing by sifting the icing sugar into a bowl and mixing with food colouring, rose essence and enough lemon juice to make a soft but not runny icing. Dip the top of each choux bun in the icing and place on the wire rack to dry. Before the icing dries completely, place a crystallised rose petal on each bun, slightly to the side.

In a small heavy saucepan boil the sugar and glucose to make a pale gold caramel. Put the

For the filling

4 egg yolks

115 g/4 oz/½ cup rose petal sugar – see p.20

3 tablespoons rose petal syrup – see p.23

80 g/3½ oz/⅞ cup plain flour

600 ml/20 oz/2 ½ cups whole milk

For the decoration

225 g/8 oz/1 ⅔ cups icing sugar

a drop or two of pink food colouring

a drop or two of culinary rose essence – see pp.14 and 15

lemon juice – see recipe

150 g/6 oz/⅔ cup crystallised rose petals or pieces

200 g/7 oz/1 scant cup granulated sugar

20 g/4 oz glucose

base of the saucepan in cold water to stop the sugar caramelising further.

Dip the side of the choux buns in the caramel and on your presentation plate make a crown of 8, then the next layer will be 7, the next 6 and so on until you reach the top choux bun. You can use more rose petals or silvered pink balls to add further decoration. *Et voilà.*

Index